Hard Sell

Hard Sell

Work and Resistance in Retail Chains

Peter Ikeler

ILR Press
an imprint of
Cornell University Press
Ithaca and London

First published 2016 by Cornell University Press

First printing, Cornell Paperbacks, 2016

Printed in the United States of America

Library of Congress Cataloging-in-Publication Data

Names: Ikeler, Peter, author.
Title: Hard sell : work and resistance in retail chains / Peter Ikeler.
Description: Ithaca ; London : ILR Press, an imprint of Cornell University Press, 2016. | ©2016 | Includes bibliographical references and index.
Identifiers: LCCN 2016013020 | ISBN 9781501702419 (cloth : alk. paper) | ISBN 9781501702426 (pbk. : alk. paper)
Subjects: LCSH: Retail trade—United States—Management. | Industrial relations—United States.
Classification: LCC HF5429.215.U6 I44 2016 | DDC 658.8/7—dc23
LC record available at http://lccn.loc.gov/2016013020

Cornell University Press strives to use environmentally responsible suppliers and materials to the fullest extent possible in the publishing of its books. Such materials include vegetable-based, low-VOC inks and acid-free papers that are recycled, totally chlorine-free, or partly composed of nonwood fibers. For further information, visit our website at www.cornellpress.cornell.edu.

Cloth printing   10 9 8 7 6 5 4 3 2 1

Paperback printing   10 9 8 7 6 5 4 3 2 1

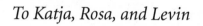

To Katja, Rosa, and Levin

Contents

Acknowledgments

This book has been more than five years in the making and has incurred many debts along the way. My interest in low-wage services as a field for union organizing first developed while at the Ruhr University in Bochum, Germany. There I learned much about European industrial relations from Luitpold Rampeltshammer, Zeynep Sezgin, Markus Hertwig, Jürgen Mittag, and Ludger Pries but also from local activists Sönke Schröder, Claus Ludwig, and Conny Dahmen.

When I returned to the United States at the end of the Great Recession I became immersed in a group of scholars at the CUNY Graduate Center who were committed to social justice and unraveling the contradictions of late-neoliberalism. Through some stroke of luck (or perhaps the wisdom of Rati Kashyap) I was assigned as a research assistant to Ruth Milkman, who served as my dedicated mentor from then on. It was she who suggested I focus on a paradigmatic industry within low-wage services and she who encouraged me to pursue a comparative study. This book owes much to her guidance, though any remaining faults are my own. Stanley Aronowitz and Phil Kasinitz, also of the CUNY Graduate Center, provided important insight about the U.S. labor movement, the history of New York retail, and the research and writing processes. Gerald Sider, an anthropologist (though he might dispute the label), continually challenged me to think outside the box, and while this work is less daring than his, it certainly benefited from his input.

Early versions, chapters, and ideas were tested on and critiqued by fellow graduate students at CUNY. David Monaghan, Melanie Lorek, Kevin Moran, Sara Martucci, and Calvin Smiley in particular read many drafts during a year-long collaborative writing group. But I also learned from discussions with Erin Michaels, Jeff Broxmeyer, Jane McAlevey, Kathleen Dunn, Jan Haldipur, Daron Howard, Tommy Wu, Ben Haber, Jamie McCallum, Fang Xu, Daniel Douglas, Sara Salman, Tom Buechele, and Luke Elliott-Negri. In sum, the intellectual environment at CUNY was vibrant and stimulating, and I thank the Graduate Center for research funds that supported the interview process. Since leaving there for SUNY Old Westbury, my thinking on this project has continued to benefit from conversations with my colleagues in the sociology department and with my students—many of whom work in retail, some even at the firms I studied.

My orientation to this project was not purely intellectual but, as the first and last chapters make clear, strategic with regard to social change. I owe much to my ongoing collaboration with a group of activists in New York City: Tom Crean, Jesse Lessinger, Alan and Frango Akrivos, Eleanor Rodgers, Eljeer Hawkins, Francesca Gomes, Margaret Collins, Bob Commike, Leon Pinsky, Elma Relihan, Cora Bergantiños, and others. Though we may not agree on every detail, our discussions over the years have greatly informed the orientation of this book.

Katja, my partner since before this book was even an idea, joined me on the path from Germany to New York to allow me to pursue a Ph.D. She engaged in countless hours of discussion on the book's subject matter, dealt with countless more hours of my silent writing, and provided vital input on how to have meaningful conversations with interview subjects. Her gifts as a teacher—which she has shared with me in so many ways—deeply influenced my research process. My parents, Roberta and Bott, and my sister, Eve, have been unflaggingly supportive, and my father, a poet, provided stylistic guidance on the final manuscript. The last year of writing was made infinitely more joyous by the arrival of our twins, Rosa and Levin. I hope they and their generation will enjoy the fruits of a revived labor movement and a postcapitalist world.

Last but not least are the seventy-five New Yorkers who sacrificed their time (a precious local commodity) to talk with me about their working lives. Much of this book speaks through their voices and is thus greatly indebted to them. To any who read this, or to others who work in similar places, I hope I have done your experience justice.

Abbreviations

AFL	American Federation of Labor
AFSCME	American Federation of State, County and Municipal Employees
AMC	Amalgamated Meat Cutters and Butcher Workmen
CIO	Congress of Industrial Organizations
CtW	Change to Win Federation
ETL	executive team leader (at Target)
HRM	human resource management
ILWU	International Longshore and Warehouse Union
IWW	Industrial Workers of the World
MAGIC	Macy's sales mantra
NAFTA	North American Free Trade Agreement
NAICS	North American Industry Classification System
NLRB	National Labor Relations Board
OUR Walmart	Organization United for Respect at Walmart
PATCO	Professional Air Traffic Controllers Organization
PDA	personal data assistant
RAP	Retail Action Project
RCIA	Retail Clerks International Association
RWDSU	Retail, Wholesale and Department Store Union

SEIU	Service Employees' International Union
STL	store team leader (at Target)
Teamsters	International Brotherhood of Teamsters
TL	team leader (at Target)
UAW	United Auto Workers
UFCW	United Food and Commercial Workers
UREA	United Retail Employees of America
URWEA	United Retail and Wholesale Employees of America
URWDSEA	United Retail, Wholesale and Department Store Employees of America

Hard Sell

1

All Quiet on the Service Front?

This book starts with a strike—almost. On June 16, 2011, more than four thousand workers at four New York Macy's stores came within hours of walking off the job. It would have been the first such action at the storied department store since 1972. Instead, in the wee hours of the morning, representatives of Local 1-S of the Retail, Wholesale and Department Store Union (RWDSU) agreed to a tepid five-year deal and called off the strike. One day later, workers at a nearby Target store in Valley Stream, New York, cast ballots in a widely watched unionization drive. Like most such elections in the last twenty years, it failed. Hopes for a beachhead of unionism in big-box retail were dashed, at least temporarily.

Shortly after these events, I began interviewing salespeople from two of the unionized Macy's stores. Opinions on the settlement were not hard to find. "We should've went out," said Jerry.[1] "It was right before Father's Day—bust their chops! We should've, but after all that we got 65 cents." Ethel felt the same: "We should've had a strike," she told me. "I think they sold out. We got a 65-cent raise the first year, but they knew we wanted a dollar, so they

---

1. This and all other workers' names have been changed to conceal their identities.

screwed us." Carol, however, was more ambivalent: "If they [the union] had said so, we would've gone on strike. But it's up to each individual, whether to show up or not. Because you are trying to live for yourself and if you are striking you never know how long that would be." Harry, a stock clerk in his early twenties, was one of these individuals. "Me personally, I still would've went to work," he said, "because if you strike you're not going to get paid. I just do what I have to do."

A few months later, when speaking with New York City Target workers, I found that some were aware of the recent drive to organize. Joan, a cashier, knew that "Valley Stream was trying to go union," and described a concerted effort by management to avoid this: "One of our executives [managers] was pulling people into rooms and telling them, 'If these people come in here, don't even bother talking to them.'" Karissa, a summertime salesperson, noted that the first time she ever heard about unions was "a week after I got back [in June 2011]. I heard about Valley Stream and they showed us a video, the HR people. I really didn't care to see the video; they pulled me away from my work section and I was like 'what am I doing here?'" Anthony, a stock clerk who had also seen the video, was wary I might be an organizer and asked for assurances to the contrary. "I heard they [unions] are trying to target the stores in the New York area," he stated, "but if they come by I'm not signing up because I don't want to be a part of it." Though many were unaware of the Valley Stream drive and some unfamiliar even with the concept of unions, several, like Joan, were clearly prounion: "We could use the union. Because what is the union supposed to do? Fight for the people that work for the company!"

Alongside fast-food, retail is among the most recognizable low-wage industries in twenty-first-century America. From *Saturday Night Live*'s Best Buy and Target skits to Walmart as the proverbial rock bottom in *Fun with Dick and Jane*, it has become synonymous with low-wage, unstable, "stopgap" work (Tannock 2001; Appelbaum, Bernhardt, and Murnane 2003; Coulter 2014). Average wages for frontline workers are 30 percent below the private-sector average, and those in general merchandise—which includes Macy's, Target, and Walmart—are 44 percent lower, at $11.23 per hour (U.S. Bureau of Labor Statistics 2014a). As might be expected, the industry is also broadly nonunion: fewer than 5 percent of retail workers are in unions today, down from more than 10 percent in 1983 (Hirsch and Macpherson 2014). On the face of it, retail thus appears ripe for organizing and the boost in wages this has historically brought. Some go further, arguing that big-box retail provides "the template of twenty-first-century capitalism" (Lichtenstein 2006) and that it is "hard to imagine a revitalized and powerful labor movement in the U.S. without a unionized Wal-Mart"—or retail sector, for that matter (Moody 2007, 234).

Yet the experiences related above suggest deeper obstacles: first and foremost, the tenacity of employer resistance; second, the timidity of many existing unions. But deeper still are the subjective hurdles faced by many workers: Why are wages so low? Why can't I afford the company's health insurance? Is management on my side? Are my coworkers? What are the alternatives? What, for that matter, is a union? From a certain standpoint, one could "impute" answers to these questions and try to relay them to workers—as could groups that aim to advance their interests. A more scientific and ultimately more democratic approach, however, is to contextualize workers' own answers within a robust description of their lived experience. If we can grasp the relationship between work and consciousness in this paradigmatic service sector, we can better assess the forces for change.

Labor Movements in Crisis and Renewal

Occurring so close in space and time, the events of June 2011 appeared to symbolize the twin dilemmas of the American labor movement: cautious conservatism in its remaining areas of strength and inability to gain traction in new ones. But the crisis of American labor is hardly new. While the slide in working-class power that began after President Reagan's crushing of the 1981 strike by the Air Traffic Controllers is well known, stagnation was evident long before, with some even pointing to the passage of the Taft-Hartley Act in 1947. By this account, it would seem that America's industrial unions, if not those in the older American Federation of Labor (AFL), began to die only shortly after their birth. The tragedy of American labor, when compared with its European counterparts, consists precisely in this belated birth, early decline, and the failure to transmit its practices to a new generation of service workers.

Plenty of ink has been spilled trying to explain labor's predicament and identify the sources of its renewal. But broadly absent is a sustained interrogation of the service labor process and how it affects workers' will to organize. In what follows, I present the highlights of this decline-and-renewal debate in order to tease out four underexamined questions. These questions, in slightly different form, were central to debates about the future of industrial unions in the 1970s and '80s; among sociologists of service work, they have received more recent attention with respect to work itself. Yet advocates of union renewal have largely sidestepped them, focusing instead on organizing tactics, union forms, or worker demographics (Bronfenbrenner et al. 1998; Clawson 2003; Cobble 1991b; Fine 2005; Milkman 2006; Ness 2005). This book attempts to unite these divided fields and, as Juravich and Bronfenbrenner admonish us, "bring the study of work back to labor studies" (2005).

Front and center in most accounts of labor's decline since the 1970s is a set of processes summed up by the word "globalization." Defined as the expansion of economic activity beyond the boundaries of nation-states, globalization has been cited time and again as the cause *tout court* of the weakening of workers' bargaining power. Alan Tonelson's *Race to the Bottom* (2002) is a primary expression of this, with Beverly Silver (2003) providing a much-needed rejoinder. In line with such expectations, unions in private-sector manufacturing—those most exposed to global competition—have suffered severe losses, declining in the United States from nearly 8 million members and a 40 percent density rate in 1973 to only 1.4 million members and 10 percent today (Hirsch and Macpherson 2014). In response, authors such as Kim Moody (1997), Kate Bronfenbrenner (2007), and Jamie McCallum (2013) have considered the utility of so-called global unions. But as Ruth Milkman (2013) points out, it is not only in globally exposed industries that U.S. unions have fallen: membership in construction and trucking—place-bound industries—has declined almost as much. Additional forces must be at work.

Industrial relations scholars cite "the emergence of a nonunion model" and attendant union resistance among U.S. employers (Kochan, Katz, and McKersie 1994). During the postwar heyday of collective bargaining firms such as Kodak, Sears, and Thompson Products honed their skills at union avoidance through a combination of welfare provision and punitive oversight (Jacoby 1997). Thomas Kochan, Harry Katz, and Robert McKersie (1994) describe a shift even within unionized firms toward "human resource management" (HRM). By the 1980s, this approach had gained enough momentum—and was bolstered by Japanese-style "lean production"—to constitute what Michael Goldfield calls a "capitalist offensive" that contributed significantly to union decline (1987, 189). To combat such maneuvers, some call for unions to pursue "rank-and-file intensive" and "comprehensive organizing" (Bronfenbrenner et al. 1998; Voss and Sherman 2000). Others consider new forms of worker organization that could circumvent employer antiunionism (Cobble 1991b; Fine 2005; Heckscher 2001).

Employers, however, do not act alone. As Moody notes, "The decline [of U.S. unions] has a definite turning point . . . the years 1980–81" (2007, 1). The "Reagan Revolution" consisted of a series of government actions that greatly augmented the power of capital over labor: financial and industrial deregulation, reduced taxes on wealth, the firing, by presidential fiat, of more than eleven thousand air traffic controllers, and the restructuring of the National Labor Relations Board (NLRB) from an ostensibly neutral body to one with a decidedly probusiness tilt. Such "reforms" did not end with Republican reign in 1992 but continued under Clinton, whose signature "achievements" were the signing of the North American Free Trade Agreement (NAFTA) and the curtailing of welfare benefits. Combined with more recent attacks on union rights in former strongholds such as Wisconsin, Michigan, and Indiana, the state (writ large) has played an important role in determining that "by the 2010s . . . the New Deal labour relations system was a dead letter" (Milkman 2013, 647). Movements for political reform, mostly local, have appeared and been further publicized by scholars such as Stephanie Luce (2004), whose study of living wage struggles helped them take center stage in the fight against inequality.

An older line of thinking also places blame on labor's doorstep— more specifically, on U.S. unions' bureaucratic leadership. As early as the 1960s Art Preis claimed that "union officials want to stifle the class struggle, not lead it" ([1964] 1972, 11). This criticism continued through the 1970s and gained renewed traction in the 1980s, as many leaders proved unwilling to combat the onslaught of concessions and plant closures (Aronowitz 1972; Bluestone and Harrison 1982; Moody 1988; Piven and Cloward 1979, 96–180). In 1995, dissatisfaction reached the upper echelons of U.S. labor, culminating in the election of John Sweeney as president of the AFL-CIO on a promise of renewed growth through organizing. Nearly two decades and a major split[2] later, this promise has not been fulfilled—some argue because of the entrenchment of "do nothing unionism" (Lopez 2004). The remedy, they assert, is rank-and-file activism that can challenge leaders and invigorate peer-to-peer organizing (Burns 2011; Early 2011; Moody 2007).

A final oft-cited cause of union decline is more secular in nature. Touted by some as "the great hope of the twentieth century" (Fourastié 1949) and by others as a force for "the end of ideology" (Bell 1960, 1973), the rise of service employment is frequently given as a reason for union decline due to the sector's supposedly less alienating conditions. Today it is hardly useful to speak of "services" as such since they constitute more than three-quarters of advanced capitalist workforces. Of the five major subgroups—health and education, retail and personal services, business and financial services, transportation, and government and security—theories of union obsolescence are clearly disproven for the first, fourth and fifth, which boast some of the highest unionization rates in the developed world.[3] But for the second and third, which encompass

2. That of the Change to Win (CtW) rival federation in 2005.
3. It is arguable that "transportation," with its material rather than interpersonal focus and long-standing traditions of conflict and unionism, more closely approximates goods production than service provision.

nearly half of U.S. workers and are less than 10 percent organized, union irrelevance appears hauntingly true. Why then are unions so broadly absent here, particularly in the low-wage sector where conditions seem to cry out for redress? Is there something intrinsic to interactive services that mitigates unionization and its seeming prerequisite, a collective, oppositional consciousness? And how are such workplaces changing? Are they tending in directions that might encourage or further inhibit worker organizing?

These are the questions this book seeks to answer. Through a focused comparison of two iconic department stores in New York City, I interrogate the organization and social relations of service work, how it evolves, and how these forces shape workers' consciousness. I integrate these findings to identify the obstacles and inroads to service-sector organizing in the United States. This is aided by the work of those who have probed these dynamics in the past. It is to a consideration of their contributions that I now turn.

Work and Consciousness

Perhaps the most well-known author to address the question of workplace consciousness is Michael Burawoy. Arguing in *Manufacturing Consent* that "conflict and consent are not primordial conditions but products of the particular organization of work," he refocused discussions of worker consciousness on the labor process (1979, 12). Work, in his view, is "relatively autonomous" from the wider social environment and its changes under monopoly capitalism largely responsible for the decline in labor militancy. Yet Burawoy's research, which involved extended participation in a Chicago-area machine shop, uncovered anything but a monolithic workplace. On the contrary, occupational divisions and the evolving character of worker-manager relations were found to differentially shape workers' attitudes and behavior. These same dimensions—work organization and employment relations—have since gained currency as the defining features of manufacturing. But there is discontinuity with services. Service-work scholars, propelled by Arlie Hochschild's (1983) concept of emotional labor and Robin Leidner's (1993) of the service triangle, have proceeded in more subjective directions and only in the last decade begun to reconsider structure (Bélanger and Edwards 2013). The challenge at hand is thus to disentangle each debate and unite their core insights.

Work Organization

For much of human history, the organization of work has been simple: one person performed all tasks needed to produce a useful thing, be it a sharpened spear, a pair of shoes, or a plate of food. Cooperation, to be sure, emerged very early but was mainly confined to large-scale hunting in preagricultural societies and large-scale construction in agricultural ones. It was only with the Industrial Revolution of the late 1700s that cooperation and a detailed division of labor became widespread. Adam Smith ([1776] 1993) was the first to recognize this; Karl Marx took the analysis further: "A large number of workers working together, at the same time, in one place (or, if you like, in the same field of labour), in order to produce the same sort of commodity under the command of the same capitalist, constitutes the starting point of capitalist production" ([1867]1976, 439). If collectivization is fundamental to the capitalist labor process, then it is surely a defining feature of its organization. Embedded within collectivized work is also the potential for domination. Control from above, or "command" as Marx puts it, thus constitutes another dimension of work. And just as collectivization makes possible but does not require control, so do both provide the necessary yet insufficient conditions for simplification. Smith, again, was the first to take note. Examining work in a pin factory, he found the complexity of tasks greatly reduced from preindustrial methods:

> One man draws out the wire, another straights it, a third cuts it, a fourth points it, a fifth grinds it at the top for receiving the head; to make the head requires two or three distinct operations; to put it on, is a peculiar business, to whiten the pins is another; it is even a trade by itself to put them into the paper; and the important business of making a pin is, in this manner, divided into about eighteen distinct operations, which, in some manufactories, are all performed by distinct hands. ([1776] 1993, 12)

Harry Braverman later described this same process as the "the separation of conception and execution" or the de-skilling of frontline work (1974, 79).

Service jobs, however, are harder to collectivize than their goods-producing counterparts. When a commodity is consumed simultaneously with its production and involves personal interaction, it can hardly be stockpiled; it also presents fewer opportunities for worker cooperation. Nevertheless, the twentieth century saw the emergence of large-scale service enterprises in health care, education, hospitality, and retail. Clearly services can be collectivized, or at least aggregated, even if unevenly. But control and complexity are more problematic. Leidner's (1993) study of fast-food servers and insurance salespeople uncovered alternate axes of control: customers, rather than simply providing "raw material" for service performance, were unpredictable agents whom managers and workers sought to regulate; in other instances, customer reports were used by managers to monitor workers. Hence the old dyad of worker-manager becomes a triad in services, with multiple pathways for alliance and conflict.

Hochschild also identified service work's unique content. Rather than manipulating things, as in goods production, or symbols, as in intellectual production, service provision "require[s] one to induce or suppress feelings in order to sustain the outward countenance that produces the proper state of mind in others" (1983, 7). She called this "emotional labor" and distinguished between "surface acting," in which workers engage in superficial encounters, and "deep acting," in which they develop long-term relationships. Though Hochschild's emphasis on the interpersonal remains largely unchallenged, the intensity of emotional labor, as well as patterns of alliance and conflict and their impact on consciousness vary widely among workplaces. They require firsthand investigation.

Employment Relations

Burawoy's (1979) study, like many before and since, showed how not simply work itself but also its embedding social relations shape consciousness. The most fundamental relation in all but a few workplaces is the wage-for-effort bargain: workers agree, often tacitly, to show up at certain times, expend energy in predetermined ways, and generally submit to employers' direction. In return they receive more or less wages, security, or comfort, and these are more variable than relations of ownership. Sanford Jacoby (1997), for example, traces the rise and persistence of American "welfare capitalism" in which large employers provided generous wages and benefits—as well as sophisticated paternalism—in order to keep unions out. Unions and collective bargaining also reveal the elasticity of wages and workplace relations. Indeed, a

central finding of *Manufacturing Consent* was that unionization
had transformed the managerial strategy of work speedup into a
fair "game" in which workers could "make out."

Since the late 1970s, however, such fairness and preemptive gen-
erosity have largely vanished. Kochan, Katz, and McKersie argue
that "concession bargaining, workplace innovations, and the rise
in the importance of nonunion human resource management systems represent a breakdown of the industrial relations system that
was shaped by New Deal labor policies and the early institution-
alization of collective bargaining during and immediately after
World War II"(1994, 21). What they call the "nonunion industrial
relations system" originally looked much like welfare capitalism.
But as union decline became more permanent, it morphed into a
low-road model epitomized by Walmart and McDonald's. Workers at Walmart and similar firms often receive sub-living wages
and have little access to benefits and almost no job security; many
also struggle—and fail—to attain full-time hours or predictable
schedules (Kalleberg 2011; Lichtenstein 2006, 2009). The decline of
organized labor thus seems to have accentuated the "mean" side
of many U.S. firms (Gordon 1996).

Services have been more central to discussions of employment
relations than to those about work organization—probably because service employers, particularly retailers, were among the
early innovators in this field. Susan Benson (1986, 143) notes
how prewar department stores purveyed "[w]elfare work [that]
included store facilities and social service programs for workers"; Jacoby (1997) details Sears's deployment of high wages,
profit sharing, and patriarchy to inculcate loyalty; and Bethany
Moreton (2009) traces the southern origins and compliance effects of Walmart's morning rituals and gendered paternalism. In
sum, service workers have often been guinea pigs for the latest

managerial trends, which typically involve altering pay, benefits, or supervisory style. But how these are arranged in individual workplaces and how they are received by workers remain open empirical questions.

How It All Evolves

Taken together, work organization and employment relations compose the total labor process that workers experience. At any given time these are relatively fixed, but a prime feature of work under capitalism is that it constantly changes. How and why this happens has been the subject of much debate. Since the 1970s, three general positions have been staked out.

Braverman (1974) put forward a radical de-skilling hypothesis that saw capitalists as increasing control through observation, routinization, and mechanization of workers' tasks. Later contributors in the same vein emphasized worker resistance to such degradation, with Richard Edwards (1979) and Burawoy (1979) identifying alternate employer strategies when de-skilling is impractical. Upgrading theorists, for their part, assert the opposite. Robert Blauner (1964) and Daniel Bell (1973) cite technological change; Michael Piore and Charles Sabel (1984) point to normative shifts in industrial relations; and lean production, or "Toyotist," enthusiasts argue that the rational interests of employers compel them to seek "high performance workplaces" whose spread raises overall skill levels (Whitfield 2000; Ohno 1988; see Dohse, Jürgens, and Malsch 1985 for a critique). Last, contingency theorists take issue with the very directionality of change. Stephen Wood (1987) and Paul Attewell (1987, 1990) question whether degradation can ever be empirically verified, Roger Penn (1986) sees frontline de-skilling as offset by growing maintenance and management staff, and

Cynthia Cockburn (1983) argues that gender, rather than job complexity, plays a major role in skill designations.

Service work has rarely been studied through the lens of these hypotheses. While Braverman included services in the purview of his theory, and even dedicated a short chapter to their investigation, both his and more recent efforts (e.g., Ritzer 1993) are empirically weak (with the exception of Curley and Royle 2013). How frontline service jobs are changing and to what extent they are becoming more skilled, less skilled, or simply more differentiated are thus broadly open questions that this book seeks to answer.

Class Consciousness

Working-class consciousness presents a different can of worms. Predicated on the social division between capitalists and workers, it has long been sought by activists as a key ingredient for progressive change. Historically, it is also on the basis of class that workers have formed the most effective unions and political parties. Michael Mann (1973) defines class consciousness as having four distinct moments:

> class *identity*—the definition of oneself as working-class, as playing a distinctive role in common with other workers in the productive process . . . class *opposition*—the perception that the capitalist and his agents constitute an enduring opponent to oneself . . . class *totality*—the acceptance of the two previous elements as the defining characteristics of (*a*) one's total social position and (*b*) the whole society in which one lives. Finally comes the conception of an *alternative society*, a goal toward which one moves through the struggle with the opponent. (1973, 13)

Ethnographers and historians critique this formulation. Rick Fantasia (1988, 11) believes it ignores the "transformative associational bonding" workers undergo in struggle, while Ira Katznelson (1986, 14–20) argues that consciousness is but one stage in a historical (and typically national) process of "class formation" (see also Thompson 1963). But to study the localized consciousness of workers not in open struggle—as most workers are most of the time—Mann's schema provides the most useful starting point, if needing some modification. First, it is unlikely for experience in a single workplace to engender views of "class totality" or of an "alternative society." Excluding these "higher levels" leaves the first two—identity and opposition. Second, Mann's "identity" has two points of reference: "with other workers" and "in the productive process." Because of this, class identity appears to consist more directly of "co-worker solidarity"—identifying the interests of colleagues with one's own—and "occupational identity"—identifying with the role one plays on the job (Cobble 1991b). This yields a three-part model of what might be termed "workplace-based" class consciousness.

Aside from overblown assertions to the contrary, the question of whether services can generate this or other forms of class consciousness has been approached only at the margins. Hochschild and others have linked the performance of emotional labor to self-alienation and feelings of inauthenticity (Hochschild 1983; Wharton 1993; Erickson and Wharton 1997; Sloan 2007). This dynamic can be extended to also limit occupational identity. For another, the triangle of service relations and the alliances they enable may also reduce workers' opposition to management (Bolton and Houlihan 2010; Leidner 1996). But the effects of sex-typing are more ambiguous. Many service jobs are explicitly gendered, with "caring labor" often defined as an extension of "feminine" duties (England 1992; Guy and Newman 2004). To the extent this ideology is effective it may hinder job identity and opposition. Where not effective, however, such "special oppression" can produce gender solidarity and opposition (Cobble 1991a; Hartmann 1981; Jones 2001). Furthermore, where employers encourage workers to have a "positive mental attitude," authoritarian supervision may be less effective than supportive, collaborative techniques (Leidner 1993; Korczynski 2002; Sherman 2007). Such "soft" management leads one to expect less opposition from workers.

These expectations about how services shape consciousness lie at the heart of this book. They are tackled in chapter 6, after the contours of work at two retailers have been fully laid out. What remains before embarking on this journey is to describe my research process—a task that occupies the rest of this chapter.

The Research Process

In early 2011 I set out to understand the experience of contemporary service workers and the chances for militancy among them. I wanted to study more than one site and hear workers' direct opinions on their jobs, workplace politics, and U.S. society. Participant observation, for all its merits, would have made these goals hard to achieve. I therefore opted to conduct a series of in-depth interviews rather than embed myself as a frontline employee. But where to start?

Of the nine major service sectors defined by the U.S. Census,[4] education and health, wholesale and retail, and professional and business services are the largest. The first are mainly in the public sector

---

4. Wholesale and retail trade, transportation and utilities, information, financial activities, professional and business services, education and health services, other services, and public administration (although transportation and utilities have high proportions of production-type jobs) (U.S. Bureau of Labor Statistics 2014d).

and because of that are highly unionized (Hirsch and Macpherson 2014). Professional and business services, though only 3 percent unionized, employ mostly professional workers whose average wages are well above the private-sector mean (U.S. Bureau of Labor Statistics 2014a, 2014d). In retail, however, fewer than 10 percent of workers are managers or professionals, and their average wages are just 63 percent of the private-sector mean (ibid.). Nearly 12 percent of all U.S. workers are employed in retail, but fewer than 5 percent of them are union members. Retail is America's largest low-wage, nonunion service industry and thus fertile terrain for the exploration of class consciousness.

Within retail I focused on department stores, and among them I studied those in New York City. Home to some of the most well-known traditional retailers, New York has only since the late 1990s been colonized by big-box and discount chains (Angotti 2008). Macy's in particular has its oldest—and in four cases unionized—stores in the city, and I chose these both because they likely resemble earlier modes of selling and because they offered a window into existing retail unionism. Among the big-box entrants to the New York market—which do not include Walmart—I chose Target for comparison. Target is the third-largest discounter after Walmart and Costco, is completely nonunion, and is seen by many as a trendsetter in the genre (Spector 2005). The uniqueness of New York's economy and workforce also made it imperative that any comparison case be in the same place (Sassen 2001). Table 1.1 displays key characteristics of both Macy's and Target for the year my research began.

Between June 2011 and August 2012 I spent several hundred hours roaming around two unionized Macy's and three nonunion Target stores, all within the five boroughs of New York. I initiated informal conversations with salespersons, stock workers and

TABLE 1.1

Selected characteristics for Macy's, Inc. and Target Corporation, 2011

	Macy's, Inc.	Target Corporation
Model	Traditional, full-line	Discount
U.S. outlets	842 (including 44 Bloomingdale's)	1,763
Employees	171,000	365,000
U.S. sales	$26.4 billion	$68.5 billion
U.S. profit (post-tax)	$1.3 billion	$2.9 billion
Profit rate	4.8%	4.3%
Sales per employee	$154,415	$187,578
Unionization	10% of national workforce	None
Sales method	Individual: some commission; personal sales goals; no cashiers	Collective: no commission; storewide sales goals; cashiers

Sources: Macy's 2012a; Target Corporation 2012b.

cashiers by asking basic questions about their jobs. If they seemed open, I invited them to a formal interview at a nearby café or park and offered $20 in return. Over the course of fourteen months, sixty-two workers (thirty-one from each company) and the president of the Macy's union local sat with me for interviews. During the summer of 2013, I interviewed an additional thirteen workers from a nonunion Macy's store in the same city. In the course of each interview I asked questions about work dynamics and conditions; about workers' feelings toward management, coworkers, and customers; and about their individual backgrounds and future plans. Each discussion was only semistructured, however, and respondents were encouraged to develop their own narratives. Table 1.2 provides basic demographics of the seventy-five workers interviewed.

TABLE 1.2
Sample characteristics, Macy's and Target New York City workers, 2011–13

	Macy's (N=44)	Target (N=31)
Job title		
Salespersons	82%	61%
Cashiers	N/A	19%
Stock clerks	9%	13%
Food servers	N/A	6%
Merchandisers	7%	N/A
Supervisors	2%	0%
Employment relations		
Union members	66%	0%
Full-time	61%	42%
Average hourly wage ($)	$11.41	$10.29
Average job tenure (years)	3.5	2.0
Worker characteristics		
Average age (years)	28	24
Primary earners	59%	35%
Women	64%	52%
Black	64%	71%
Asian	14%	3%
Latino	7%	13%
White	16%	13%
Foreign-born	34%	45%

Overview

This story unfolds in the next six chapters. Chapter 2 provides a historical overview of retail trade and unionism since the early twentieth century. It shows how large firms developed relatively late in retail and how, because of this, sales work did not become highly collectivized until after World War II. Unionism, for its part, began among small, independent retailers but shifted to chain and department stores in the 1930s and '40s, making rapid gains along with the Congress of Industrial Organizations (CIO) upsurge. But these gains proved ephemeral, and retail unionism never achieved the industry-wide clout of its mass-production peers. The assault on labor since the 1980s and the rise of nonunion discounters have placed sales workers in an increasingly precarious and hostile organizing environment.

Chapter 3 begins my comparison of Macy's and Target, examining the organization of sales work at these two iconic retailers. They display starkly different processes. Macy's was specialized, decentralized, and competitive, with many jobs requiring workers to apply detailed product knowledge. Target, by contrast, was routinized and collectivized, with few jobs requiring any measurable or transferable skills. I argue that these represent two distinct modes of selling: "eroded craft" at Macy's and "service Toyotism" at Target.

In chapter 4 I discuss the social relations that underpinned and enabled these regimes. Macy's had an adversarial culture where authoritarian supervision and distrust of managers were common. Target, for its part, was more "harmonious": it cultivated a Disney-infused teamwork that was deliberately antiunion and often enough worked. While both were low-wage employers that paid most workers less than twelve dollars an hour, Target, surprisingly, had a two-dollar higher wage floor than unionized Macy's. The caveat was that Macy's wages ranged much higher, and its unionized workers had far more security than their nonunion peers. Altogether, I argue that Macy's adversarialism was part and parcel of its semiskilled, eroded craft model in which what workers did was less understood by managers. In parallel fashion, Target's "teamwork" was both an enabler and result of its de-skilled sales process in which managerial control was embedded in the very structure of work.

Chapter 5 combines the results of the preceding chapters to assess how sales work has changed and where it is heading. Using chapter 2 as historical context and Macy's and Target as proxies for older and newer sales models, I interrogate the grand hypotheses of labor process theory as they pertain to department stores. Comparing transformations in work organization, employment relations, and worker characteristics, I argue that emotional labor has undergone de-skilling, that this has been accompanied by a shift from adversarialism to paternalism, and that the transition from a "primary" workforce of self-supporting adults to a "secondary" one of students and dependents has been an integral part of these changes. I then outline an emerging regime of "contingent control" in low-wage workplaces. Building upon Edwards's (1979) influential schema, I identify four features of this regime and pinpoint Target as ideal-typical, unionized Macy's as a more distant predecessor, and nonunion Macy's as a transitional case.

In chapter 6 I turn to the question of class consciousness. I explore service workers' subjectivity through a four-part prism of job identity, solidarity, opposition, and union support. Unionized Macy's workers, as might be expected, showed greater identity and opposition and were more prounion than their nonunion peers at either firm. But solidarity was much stronger at Target. I attribute this to Target's collectivized, team-based model as compared with Macy's individualized and competitive one. There was little to support the idea that service work dulls class consciousness in and of itself, since Macy's workers—union and nonunion—were more class conscious while engaging in deeper acting and more high-stakes interactions with customers. Jobs at both firms had a clear gender gradient, but this created few differential attitudes, while Target's softer managerial style seemed to mollify worker resistance.

In the concluding chapter I return to the question of struggle, confronting the promises and challenges of organizing service workplaces in the twenty-first century. The main obstacles, I argue, are fierce employer resistance and limited structural power, which has been further eroded by de-skilling. Yet counteracting forces are also at work. The routinization of sales is entwined with collectivization, which at Target engendered heightened solidarity—a key factor in successful organizing. Furthermore, contingent control produces new grievances around insecurity that unions can take up—and some already have. Unionized Macy's, however, exposes the shortcomings of many existing unions, as well as their indifferent attitude toward many younger members. Insofar as services are tending toward collectivized, precarious, and paternalist regimes, it seems that unions must rethink not only their tactics and organizing models but also the content of their appeals and the definition of membership. The burgeoning campaigns to raise wages and respect at Walmart and fast-food chains show that this process has already begun. But the pathway to unionism in low-wage services can only be aided by a deeper understanding of workers' lived experience, which this book provides.

2

The Making of Big-Box Retail

> Capitalism can reproduce itself only by an incessant
> accumulation which develops as a mass production
> and consumption of commodities, a phenomenon
> generalized to embrace the sum total of activities of
> social life.
>
> *Michel Aglietta (1979, 81)*

In twenty-first-century America, most of us know retail as a generic shopping experience that typically takes place in big-box suburban malls. Most of us are also aware that working in retail is often low-paid, precarious, and nonunion. Some, such as Nelson Lichtenstein (2006, 2009), argue not only that retail epitomizes America's "bad jobs" phenomenon but that retailers have played an outsized role in spreading them since the 1970s. Was this all inevitable? Were retail jobs predestined to be low-wage, insecure, and nonunion? Or are these the contingent outcomes of twentieth-century history? This chapter argues the latter by tracing the development of the industry, its labor practices, and retail unions since the late nineteenth century.

An undertaking such as this requires some analytic guideposts and periodization. For these I turn to the influential regulation school of political economy, exemplified by the work of Michel

Aglietta (1979), Bob Jessop (1982), and Alain Lipietz (1989). Regulation theorists argue for the existence of long-run periods of growth ("regimes of accumulation") based on particular modes of extracting and realizing value. These stable thirty- to-forty year stretches are made possible, they say, by supportive state policies and social norms ("modes of regulation") but are bookended by acute phases of turmoil and change when the latter no longer suit the former. According to Aglietta, the greatest historical divide lies between the "extensive" and the "intensive" regimes of accumulation (71). The first, from the Civil War to the late 1920s, consisted in an expansion of labor-intensive manufacturing and a decline of independent ownership. Taylorism, based on the ideas of Frederick W. Taylor, came to the fore during the second half of this period as a method of extracting greater value from workers by routinizing their tasks, but because wages remained low, they had limited capacity to consume. This limit is often cited as a main cause of the Great Depression, which itself is credited with the rise of the New Deal and industrial unionism in the United States. Emerging from this tumult in 1945 was a new regime often referred to as "Fordism": assembly-line technology and widespread unionization paired with higher wages and mass consumption for many industrial workers. This regime underwent its own crisis in the 1970s and transitioned toward what many call "neoliberalism" in the 1980s—a regime that encapsulates trends observed during the late twentieth and early twenty-first centuries, including wage stagnation, globalization, and de-unionization (Harvey 2005).

Here I employ this four-part periodization and the concepts of the regulation school to chart U.S. retail's evolution. Within each phase, I focus on the structure of the industry, the organization of selling, and retail unionism. The story that emerges is of an industry late to the game of concentration, collectivization, and rationalization but one that caught up rapidly in the 1930s and '40s. Retail unions, though held back by minimal disruptive power, made impressive advances in certain times and subsectors. However, their strategic missteps—and those of the wider labor movement—contributed to retail's predominantly low-road, nonunion status today, enabling the rise of what I describe in chapter 5 as contingent control.

The Rise of Capitalist Retailing

If capitalist industry, properly understood, consists in large-scale organizations producing for a profit, then capitalist retailing arose relatively late. As recently as 1929 independently owned stores employing just a handful of clerks (and sometimes none) accounted for 89 percent of stores and 70 percent of sales (Lebhar 1952, 63). Ronald Coase once described corporations as "lumps of butter coagulating in a pail of buttermilk" (quoted in Hoopes 2006, 85); by this metric, American retail was still largely milk at the end of the extensive regime of accumulation—one that had congealed most manufacturing industries into solid butter.

Nevertheless, tendencies toward concentration and large-scale organization were evident. These could be seen most clearly in the urban department stores that catered to the elite and upper-middle classes; in large chains such as A&P (groceries), J.C. Penney (dry goods), and Woolworth's (variety); and in mail-order houses, represented by Sears Roebuck and Montgomery Ward. Numerically, however, small owners predominated before the Great Depression. Hundreds of thousands of mom-and-pop shops offered everything from groceries to clothing to musical instruments. According to Godfrey Lebhar, each one "specializes in particular lines of merchandise, occupies relatively small space, has limited capital, employs few, if any, workers and does such a small volume of business that their ability to stay in the picture for more than a few years is highly questionable" (1952, 3).

Department stores, when they burst upon the scene in the late nineteenth century, were "a new kind of store" (Benson 1986, 12). They eschewed specialization to a narrow range of goods and did not allow haggling and bargaining or buying on credit. Diversification, the "one-price system," and sales on a cash-and-carry rather than credit basis were the innovations that allowed them to achieve economies of scale (ibid., 15; Leach 1993, 23). But department stores were not for everyone. These "palaces of consumption" served what Thorstein Veblen (1899) called "the leisure class"—the upper stratum of consumers.

Emerging chains took a different tack. Arising primarily in groceries, drugs, and "variety" (five-and-ten-cent general merchandise), these tapped the demand of America's growing urban working class. Comparing sales growth between J.C. Penney (a national chain) and Macy's (a single department store), Lebhar found that both reached the same sales volume in 1921. But "whereas the department store, operating under a single roof, had required 63 years to reach that point . . . the chain-store company operating under a number of separate roofs scattered over a wide area in communities far smaller than New York, had reached the same point in only nineteen years" (1952, 13). The advantages of the chain model were clear enough by the 1920s that Macy's and its peers began opening branch stores and combining into national holding companies (10).

The third form of concentration was the mail-order house. "Until 1920," writes Jacoby, "more than half the U.S. population still lived in rural areas, where Sears made most of its sales. Its mail-order catalogues offered everything a farm family might need, from furniture to farm implements to shoes" (1997, 95). Size and scope allowed these firms to undercut many small-town general stores, in turn making them targets of antichain agitation in the 1920s and '30s (100–102). Yet it was Sears's shift to store-front retailing that set the stage for its preeminence in the postwar era.

A PREREQUISITE FOR restructuring work in any trade is scale: only when workers are brought under one roof, physically or institutionally, is it possible to subdivide and reallocate their tasks. But the process of such division starts from a historically given status quo. In the early twentieth century, this was undifferentiated clerking labor in small, independent stores.

The work of early clerks was grueling and multifaceted, but their skills were learned mainly on the job and did not require formal training. A typical day might last fifteen hours, and, according to George Kirstein, "a 112-hour work week was common." "In addition to that awesome schedule," he continues, "it was not unusual for an unmarried clerk to sleep on the counter at the store in order to wait on whatever trade might chance to come by night" (1950, 6). Most goods were kept behind counters, and the clerk then retrieved, discussed, packaged, and wrapped them for customers. In addition to sales tasks, small-store clerks also performed myriad maintenance duties. One employee manual from 1850 states, "Store must be swept; counters, base shelves and showcases dusted; lamps trimmed, filled and chimneys cleaned; pens made; doors and windows opened; a pail of water, also a bucket of coal brought in before breakfast (if there is time to do so) and attend to customers who call" (quoted in Kirstein 1950, 5). Nonowner clerks exploded as a category from 32,000 in 1880 to 2.3 million in 1930 (Benson 1986, app. A). Women, though a minority, made up a considerable and growing portion of this workforce, expanding from 24 to 30 percent during this same stretch (ibid.). Yet it was in department and chain stores, rather than mom-and-pop shops, where selling received a lasting "feminine" designation.

"The unique element in department-store labor policy," writes Benson, "was the encouragement of skilled selling: the use of trained salesclerks to increase the size and number of sales transactions through merchandise information and sales psychology" (1986, 125). C. Wright Mills confirms this picture by describing a varied set of tasks that allowed "salesgirls" to develop "a range of sales personalities" from the "interplay of individual with the store and the flow of customers" (1951, 174). William Leach, in his history of American consumer culture, notes that the first School of Retailing (founded in 1919 at the behest of New York department stores) aimed "to teach retailing . . . with the overall intention of upgrading saleswork into 'skilled labor'" (1993, 159). In their expansionary phase department stores created a new, feminized occupation—the retail salesclerk—that had previously existed only in independent or petty-proprietor forms (Kirstein 1950, 6–14). Given the industry's upscale orientation (in contrast to early chains), personalized service was a key component of competition. The absence of ubiquitous branding and advertising, which Mills (1951, 179) later saw as "centralizing and rationalizing" sales work, combined with store designs that "separate[ed] goods from customers," required clerks to be "skilled workers, whose expertise and training were highly valued" (Opler 2007, 81). "[W]ithout the salespeople's knowledge of the stock on hand," writes Daniel Opler, "the stores would immediately cease to operate, since customers could not gain access to goods" (ibid.).

Clerks in early department stores were not free from external control. Prices were fixed by the employer; output was monitored by buyers and "floorwalkers," providing cause for reprimand if it was too low (Mills 1951, 170); and "dress codes enforced 'a defined and appropriate 'class distinction' between the customer and the assistant [clerk]'" (Benson 1986, 140). Employers also sought to elicit consent by providing health care, company unions, and leisure facilities (ibid., 142–46; Jacoby 1997, 95–142). But despite this, significant training was often required for salespersons to competently fill their roles. Two main indices of skill—complexity and autonomy—were clearly in evidence even if their socially determined counterparts—status and pay—were not. Though the salesperson's job was not accompanied by the lore (and pay) of the carpenter or machinist, its features nonetheless define it as a form of craft work, not yet exposed to the simplifying tendencies of Taylorism, Fordism, or Toyotism.

Such simplification came earlier for chain store workers. At the start of the twentieth century, "grocery chains had taken the lead in applying scientific management by standardizing stores" (Levinson 2011, 62). "By the interwar period," states Susan Strasser, "A&P managers filled out standardized order sheets twice a week to be processed at warehouses that arranged the goods in the order they were listed"; similar procedures were already in place at other chains (2006, 46). Yet these clerks still "stood behind counters and retrieved goods," much like their small-shop counterparts (49). Five-and-dimes, typified by Woolworth's and S.S. Kresge, simplified tasks more thoroughly through the use of self-service: "Customers carried baskets through a maze of aisles that exposed them to all the merchandise, and they exited at the checkout stands" (51). Five-and-dime clerks were also typically women, as indicated by Frank Woolworth himself: "When a clerk gets so good *she* can get a better wage elsewhere, let *her* go—for it does not require skilled and experienced sales*ladies* to sell our goods. You can get good honest *girls* at from $2 to $3 per week and I would not give $3.50" (quoted in Strasser 2006, 31, emphasis added).

At mail-order plants, not only were "many of the jobs held by women," as at Woolworth's, but they were also routinized and mechanized to the level of a Fordist factory (Jacoby 1997, 97). "After the post office delivered the orders in huge sacks," writes Jacoby of Sears's processing plants in the 1910s, "they were sent through a device that date-stamped each envelope and slit it open at the rate of 450 envelopes per minute. Then the money was removed, the order was scrutinized to determine if special handling was required, and it went to the scribing department, where lading bills and box labels were printed.... To quicken the flow, heavy use was made of horizontal conveyors, vertical belts, and spiral chutes" (96). If pre-Depression chain stores evinced Taylorist patterns of simplification, mail-order plants had already made the leap to Fordism: "the integration of different segments of the labour process by a system of conveyors and handling devices" whereby "the individual worker . . . los[es] all control over his work rhythm" (Aglietta 1979, 118). At Sears and Ward's, however, it was primarily *her* work rhythm that was usurped.

PRIOR TO 1930 RETAIL unionism remained modest and local. It advanced from two different fronts and made its greatest gains among small shops, but these were modest at best. As the 1920s and the American economy wound down, the Retail Clerks International Association (RCIA)[1] and the Amalgamated Meat Cutters and Butcher Workmen (AMC) claimed fewer than twenty thousand

1. Prior to its 1944 convention, this organization was known as the Retail Clerks International Protective Association (RCIPA). For the sake of simplicity, I use its later name throughout.

retail members between them, in an industry that employed nearly two and a half million (Kirstein 1950, 217; Brody 1964, 106).

The RCIA, founded in 1890, began with only 288 members spread across seven locals in the Midwest. In thirteen years, however, it grew to 40,000 on a tide of widespread labor insurgency. Making use of consumer boycotts and the union label, RCIA fought tenaciously for "early closing" in city after city, achieving success when a majority of local merchants agreed to shorten hours (Kirstein 1950, 15). But many clerks saw little point in maintaining membership after this was achieved. Despite RCIA's involvement in several strikes in the 1910s,[2] its membership declined from 40,000 in 1903 to only 5,000 in 1933 (ibid., 42–50, 217; Harrington 1962, 7).

The second front came from skilled meat cutters organized by the AMC. These "butcher workmen" challenged the RCIA for jurisdiction and received some leeway but were restricted by the AFL leadership to organizing workers "exclusively employed at meat cutting and meat service" in nonchain grocery stores (Brody 1964, 29). Privileged with greater labor-market leverage than semiskilled clerks, the AMC swelled its retail ranks to ten thousand in 1920 by "mak[ing] membership a condition of employment" and putting "[p]ressure on employers [to] bring in almost all eligible men within the jurisdiction" (110).

In sum, while retail trade expanded rapidly during the phase of extensive accumulation, firm concentration and workplace rationalization remained relatively minor, though growing, trends. Unions organized only a small minority (i.e., fewer than one-tenth) of retail workers and, despite impressive short-term gains,

---

2. Including one in 1913 of more than four thousand predominantly female department store workers in Buffalo, New York.

were largely restricted to guerrilla warfare against the morass of petty employers. In the 1930s and '40s, the industry rapidly changed, and with it retail unions would achieve hitherto unseen breadth and influence.

Turmoil and Transition

Most explanations for the fallout of the 1930s cite an imbalance between production on the one hand and consumption on the other. Regulation theorists describe this as an overproduction of capital relative to consumer goods and point to the rise of unionism as the force that boosted working-class demand and helped stabilize American capitalism (Aglietta 1979, 94–95). Retail would undergo dramatic expansion and rationalization as the main conduit for this mass consumption, with chains playing an outsized role.

Chain stores grew during the Depression. In 1929, they accounted for 22 percent of all retail sales; by 1939 they accounted for 24 percent. But aggregate figures mask more rapid shifts in individual subsectors. Chain department stores increased their sales share from 15 to 43 percent during the same stretch and their share of stores from 60 to 94 percent. Chain drug stores and those in the "all other" food category captured an additional 5 percent of sales and shoe stores 10 percent (Lebhar 1952, 63). Individual firms plowed ahead at even greater speeds. Sears grew from 319 stores to nearly 600 between 1929 and 1940, Walgreen's from 397 to 489, J.C. Penney from 1,395 to 1,586, and Woolworth's from 1,825 to 2,027 (41, 17, 13, 34).

Small merchants fought the chains, however. Threatened with becoming a "nation of clerks," their movement gained momentum from enthusiastic Southern radio hosts and made headway

(Moreton 2009, 84; Levinson 2011, 119). "Between 1931 and 1937," writes Lichtenstein, "twenty-six states . . . enacted tax and license laws that attempted to curb or stop the growth of chain stores" (2009, 55). In 1936 Congress passed the Robinson-Patman Act preventing wholesalers from offering lower prices to chains, and two New Deal programs (the Agricultural Adjustment Act and the National Recovery Administration) favored independent stores by prohibiting price-cutting (Levinson 2011, 141–43). As the 1930s waned and war preparations began, however, the urgency of anti-chain activism receded while chain stores regrouped to challenge legislation. Yet this last gasp of small-business opposition "cast a long shadow" that enabled unions to organize chains and informed the later marketing strategies of discounters (Lichtenstein 2009, 55; see also Moreton 2009).

SELF-SERVICE WAS AMONG the innovations pioneered by chain retailers. It reduced the salesperson's role to that of either stock clerk or cashier. The first known supermarket—King Kullen of Queens, New York—offered five hundred items, was quadruple the size, and reaped ten times the sales of typical small groceries. The key to its success was low investment per sale: "relying on self-service and keeping the staff small," combined with savings on equipment and inventory (Levinson 2011, 129).

Sears took a different tack. Rather than simplifying tasks through self-service, it retooled employee relations and its market orientation. In contrast to urban department stores, such as Macy's and Marshall Field's—which marketed themselves toward an upscale, largely female clientele and employed, on average, workforces that were two-thirds women—Sears offered "middle-brand, middle-quality products for the middle-class" and employed a sales force that was two-thirds male (Lichtenstein 2009, 17; Jacoby 1997,

103). Not only did Sears practice occupational sex-typing, reserving higher-commission jobs for men; it also employed a larger share of part-time workers than did traditional department stores. Payroll costs were reduced by Sears's denial of benefits to those working less than twenty hours a week, while full-time workers received above average pay, profit sharing, paid vacation time, and health insurance (Jacoby 1997, 105, 128).

Traditional department stores underwent fewer internal changes during the Depression and war years. Though parts of their welfare schemes were dropped in the face of slumping demand, rarely did these stores significantly modify the structure or relations of work. As Benson notes, department stores' "encouragement of skilled selling . . . contrasted with self-service schemes, which department stores shunned before World War II" (1986, 125). Similarly, work reorganization was minimal to nonexistent among small proprietors, lacking as they did the requisite scale; many simply went bankrupt in the 1930s.

LIKE OTHERS AT the time, retail workers experienced the first years of the Depression as a demobilizing shock. In 1933 the RCIA was only five thousand strong and its leadership "small and without any aggressive organizational plans" (Harrington 1962, 7). The AMC was in a better position, counting nearly eleven thousand retail meat cutters among its members, but this represented only about 10 percent of that national workforce (Brody 1964, 121). It was the New Deal and the formation of the CIO that provided the impetus to massive new organizing, splitting the RCIA in the process. By its late 1940s peak, the CIO-affiliated RWDSU counted ninety thousand members, the RCIA nearly two hundred thousand, and the AMC fifty thousand in retail (Kirstein 1950, 217). The pathways to this growth, however, were not straightforward: they were punctuated by strikes, struggles, and strategic missteps.

In 1934 workers at New York City's Klein's and Ohrbach's stores struck unsuccessfully for union recognition. The militancy displayed by their predominantly female and immigrant workforce inspired a wave of action by New York locals of the RCIA that culminated in their secession (Opler 2007, 13–43). Ten of these were granted a CIO charter in 1937 to become the United Retail Employees of America (UREA, later RWDSU)[3] and made an early breakthrough at Hearn's department store, negotiating a contract without a strike (Kirstein 1950, 77). RWDSU then rapidly signed contracts at department stores across the city and the Northeast as many employers dropped their resistance in the face of widespread industrial upheaval. But conflict arose at five-and-dimes in Detroit and New York, where saleswomen staged sit-down strikes in 1937 (Frank 2001). Though these did not yield lasting gains, a 1941 strike by already-organized Gimbel's workers did, setting the pattern of a forty-hour workweek across New York City department stores (Opler 2007, 105–15). Strikes at Chicago's Montgomery Ward in 1942 and 1944 proved less fruitful. Despite favorable intervention by the government, both ended in defeat, and the ensuing squabbling, combined with anti-Communist tension after the passage of the Taft-Hartley Act, led to splits within RWDSU that ended its meteoric growth. Jacoby argues that the focus on Ward's was an error "that depleted the union's treasury before it could take on Sears" (1997, 114).

3. The UREA was successively renamed United Retail and Wholesale Employees of America (URWEA), United Retail, Wholesale and Department Store Employees of America (URWDSEA), and finally, RWDSU. For the sake of simplicity, I refer to this union as RWDSU, even when discussing its pre-1946 history.

The RCIA operated in something of a parallel universe. Shortly after the 1937 split it chartered a local in San Francisco and signed a one-year, multiemployer contract that provided a beachhead for organizing West Coast department stores (Kirstein 1950, 99). The RCIA also focused heavily on groceries. Chain grocers had long been impenetrable to organizing, but in the context of the late 1930s upsurge their resistance ebbed. A watershed neutrality agreement was signed with A&P in 1938 in return for the AFL's opposition to planned federal taxes on chains (Levinson 2011, 189). Though not a collective bargaining agreement, it led "almost immediately" to the signing of such contracts in several cities (190). By 1939, RCIA's membership was twenty times its 1933 count and nearly doubled again in the 1940s through growth among grocery chains (Harrington 1962, 7–8; Mayo 1993, 184). At the close of the 1940s fortune tilted inexorably toward the RCIA with the acquisition of former RWDSU department store locals in Philadelphia, Boston, and Buffalo (Kirstein 1950, 103). In the struggle to organize U.S. retail, the AFL had clearly beaten the CIO.

Or had it? The early 1950s saw the high-water mark of American unionism, yet even at this peak only one in ten retail workers was unionized (Kirstein 1950, 105; Estey 1955). Why such minimal density in contrast to heavy industry? Much of the answer lies in the structure of retail, where "there is no 'jugular vein,' no single area of concentration comparable to auto in Detroit or steel in the Pittsburgh area" (Harrington 1962, 3). But part of the answer also lies with events. Had RWDSU achieved contracts at Montgomery Ward or targeted Sears instead, the infighting that the Ward's loss intensified might have been avoided; furthermore, a basis for mass unionism among chain department stores could have been gained. The passage of Taft-Hartley and its enforcement inside RWDSU were also not foregone conclusions: had either been prevented, the union might not have splintered. In either case, retail's decentralized structure did not prevent impressive organizing among grocers and department stores and does not do so now.

Fordist Mass Consumption

"Fordism," writes Aglietta, "created a norm of working-class consumption" based on "*standardized housing* . . . and the *automobile*" (1979, 158, 159, emphasis in original). Between 1950 and 1980, retail rode these trends to become radically transformed— enough so that Barry Bluestone et al. (1981) could refer to a "retail revolution." Concentration was a dominant feature, led by both chain and traditional department stores, while homogenization was another, as most firms aimed at the "middle market" of home-owning, car-driving consumers. But some also targeted niche markets.

In 1967 the top five "department store" firms[4] accounted for 26 percent of general merchandise sales; by 1977 it was 52 percent (Bluestone et al., 1981, 49). Between 1963 and 1977, department store chains (Sears, J.C. Penney, etc.) increased their sales more than threefold, holding companies of traditional department stores almost fivefold, and discount stores by five and a half-fold (50). Discounters alone grew from $2 billion in sales in 1960 to $39.2 billion in 1977, at which point firms with fifty or more stores accounted for 58 percent of sales (19–21). This marked concentration came at the expense of independent stores.

---

4. Bluestone et al.'s (1981, 4) definition is somewhat eclectic, including what they term "specialty stores" (mostly in clothing and apparel) alongside the standard full-line and discount department stores.

Sears led the pack by eschewing the elite and female-centered strategy of traditional department stores while using its buying power to undercut independents (Jacoby 1997, 99–100; Bluestone et al. 1981, 16). The company grew substantially during the post-war boom from 617 stores in 1941 to "859 retail outlets . . . plus 2,920 other sales facilities and independent catalogue merchants" in 1976 (Bluestone et al. 1981, 16; Lebhar 1952, 41). Although Sears was a prime force for market homogenization, it was not the only one. Many traditional department stores opened suburban branches with scaled-down offerings (Cohen 2003, 273), grocery chains offered wide varieties in large, car-accessible buildings (Mayo 1993, 187), and discounters used these same innovations to perfect mass general merchandising (Strasser 2006).

Although in the 1950s "discount department store[s] posed no threat . . . by 1965 they were able to surpass in sales volume all of the conventional mode department stores combined" (Bluestone et al. 1981, 18). Target, Walmart, Woolco, and Kmart were all founded in 1962; Target began in Roseville, Minnesota, when soon-to-be Dayton-Hudson[5] launched the plan of one of its managers. It grew to 49 stores in 1975 and reaped $511 million in sales, surpassing Dayton-Hudson's full-line stores in revenue (Rowley 2003; Target Corporation 2012a). By the same year, Walmart had nearly 100 stores concentrated around its Ozarks homeland; Woolco had approximately 300; and Kmart topped them all with 1,254 stores (Bluestone et al. 1981, 19). The age of the discount store and the hyper-homogenization of the U.S. market had arrived.

Yet a simultaneous trend toward segmentation was also beginning. Catering to new identities emerging from the civil rights,

---

5. Minneapolis-based Dayton's merged with Detroit-based Hudson's in 1969 to form department store holding company Dayton-Hudson.

gay rights, women's liberation, and student antiwar movements, advertisers and retailers began what Cohen (2003, 292) calls "segmenting the mass": selling different products, or the same ones with different appeals, to different consumers. Bloomingdale's, a formerly staid department store, reoriented itself toward fashion-conscious youth, while specialty shops such as The Gap proliferated and "rode the wave of youth rebellion, a sexual revolution, and a revolution of rising incomes and expectations" (Zukin 2004, 127–28). As identity-specific alternatives to mass-market chains, specialty stores presaged the consumption side of neoliberalism, which came into its own in the 1980s.

BETWEEN 1950 AND 1980, RETAIL employment inched upwards from 10 to 11 percent of the U.S. workforce. The larger service sector expanded from 62 to 73 percent, while the goods-producing sector shrank from 38 to 27 percent (U.S. Bureau of Labor Statistics 2014a). Thus although retail grew, it did not grow as fast as services overall. A countervailing process—self-service sales—was at work. But this was not applied uniformly: it took hold first in supermarkets, then spread to department stores, yet labor-intensive models remained. Gender divisions were also used by many employers to weld compliant workforces.

Supermarkets were the first to move toward self-service. Whereas clerks had once waited on customers individually, in supermarkets large, organized displays allowed customers to select goods themselves while clerks stocked, cleaned, and processed payment (Strasser 2006, 51). Marc Levinson (2011, 129) estimates that the ensuing labor reduction accounted for "a stunning 56 percent return on capital" at the first King Kullen supermarket and John Walsh (1991, 461) identifies electronic scanning as a further innovation that "increased checker productivity [by] 12–14%."

Full-line department stores applied these techniques less extensively. Yet "[a]t Gimbel's in 1949 managers redesigned most of their departments. . . to allow[. . .] customers direct access to samples of merchandise without going through salespeople" (Opler 2007, 180). Suburban branches also "limit[ed] the number of salespeople needed by depending more on customer self-service," and increased their share of part-time, female employees (Cohen 2003, 283). "As the department stores established branches," writes Cohen, "they increasingly turned to suburban housewives as retail clerks" (2003, 283; also Opler 2007, 178). Sears also favored "men for full-time jobs," considering "'housewives' to be the most desirable part-timers"; many salesmen responded by ostracizing female colleagues "to preserve these lucrative jobs for other males" (Jacoby 1997, 103–5).

Discounters, however, cut costs more than Sears. Comparing wage bills in the 1970s, Bluestone et al. (1981, 30) estimated that discounters' payroll accounted for 11–13 percent of annual sales, compared with 12–14 percent at Sears and Ward's, 16–25 percent at traditional department stores, and 16–27 percent among specialty stores. The mechanisms behind these savings were, as at supermarkets, self-service and electronic scanning, which Thomas Adams argues "eviscerated much of the workplace camaraderie [and] atomized their workforce[s]" (2006, 215).

Last was the relative upgrading of sales work in specialty stores. Independent boutiques, upscale department stores (e.g., Bloomingdale's, Neiman Marcus), and clothing chains (e.g., The Gap, Abercrombie and Fitch) distinguished themselves by providing more rather than less service alongside higher-quality merchandise. "[G]eared toward consumers who are willing to pay higher prices for merchandise in order to obtain more service," wrote Bluestone et al., specialty store "managers prefer to hire sales personnel who have had previous sales experience or who present a personal style which fits the store's image" (1981, 28). At that time, they estimated specialty stores to have, on average, "full-time majority" workforces, in contrast to the part-time majorities of all other types (30).

In sum, changes in sales work during the Fordist era largely followed those of industry concentration. While grocery chains and chain and nonchain department stores turned increasingly to self-service and its attendant de-skilling, specialty stores pursued service upgrading. The latter, however, remained a small dot on the retail landscape, and the niche-market basis of their labor practices was already being undermined by a new wave of concentration.

"THE MASSIVE DEVELOPMENT of collective bargaining," writes Aglietta, "was indissolubly connected with the rise of Fordism" (1979, 189–90). The thirty years from 1950 to 1980 saw the greatest stability and influence for American trade unions, which conspicuously coincided with lowered inequality and rising living standards (Cowie and Salvatore 2008; Piketty 2014). Where were retail unions in all of this?

In 1954, half a million retail workers belonged to six different unions: the RCIA (246,500), the AMC (120,000), and the RWDSU (80,000), as well as smaller numbers in the International Brotherhood of Teamsters, the Service Employees' International Union (SEIU), and the Amalgamated Clothing Workers (Estey 1955, 560). Given that retail then employed five million individuals, this yields a density rate of about 10 percent (U.S. Bureau of Labor Statistics 2014a). In New York City, the situation was more favorable: five of the above unions (all except SEIU) claimed 90,000 members, with 54,000 in the RWDSU alone (Estey 1955, 562). This suggests a retail union density of about 30 percent in the city. By 1983, the national rate was nearly unchanged at 10.7 percent (Hirsch and Macpherson 2014), but in the late 1960s it likely reached 15 percent.[6] The primary vehicles were the RCIA and AMC, which merged to form the United Food and Commercial Workers (UFCW) in 1979.

Groceries provided a bulwark of retail unionism. By 1955, 60 percent of RCIA's membership was employed there, and in 1983 grocery unionization stood at 31 percent—triple the density for retail overall (Mayo 1993, 185; Hirsch and Macpherson 2014). How was this achieved? James Mayo points to accretion clauses: "Such a clause secured unionization for any new stores that the chain opened in the union's area, and shop rules were automatically implemented. As grocery management used new supermarkets to increase profits, the union movement increasingly ensured that their workers followed those profits and shared them" (1993, 186). This form of organizing had clear precedents in the repertoire of pre-New Deal AFL unions, but Milkman (2004–5) argues that RCIA's dependence on accretion clauses may have bred long-run complacency.

If RCIA dominated groceries, RWDSU dominated New York. Union density among the city's retail workforce rivaled that among the entire national workforce in the 1950s, grounded by left-leaning department store locals. Seven of these had separated from the RWDSU in 1948, and six (minus Macy's Local 1-S) had joined New York's District 65, "the largest left union in the city" (Freeman 2000, 89). In 1954, these erstwhile locals rejoined

6. In 1966, RCIA had 552,000 members (Mayo 1993, 224); given that the AMC's retail membership was then approximately 300,000 (ibid.; Brody 1964, 243), and holding the membership of the other four unions constant, this suggests a total membership of around 990,000 within a retail workforce 6.5 million strong, for a density rate of about 15 percent (U.S. Bureau of Labor Statistics, Current Employment Statistics 2014a).

RWDSU and embarked on a four-year drive to organize suburban branch stores. Although "District 65 adapted its organizing strategies, de-emphasizing its militant past and reaching out to women workers," this hard-fought campaign failed (Ziskind 2003, 55). Part-time employees proved unreceptive to union overtures, and struggles simply for access to shopping centers proved insurmountable (Cohen 2003, 283). Macy's Local 1-S was more successful, organizing the company's branch stores in the Bronx, White Plains, and Queens in addition to its Manhattan flagship, and chalking up steady wage gains at all four.[7]

On the whole, U.S. retail unions bucked the national trend of slow decline from the early 1950s to the Reagan era, reaching their greatest overall density in the late 1960s or early '70s. But this peak was never as high as those attained in heavy industry, construction, or later in the public sector. Furthermore, it was overwhelmingly concentrated in groceries. Though significant gains were achieved at individual stores and across some urban regions, a national pattern of "mature" collective bargaining never emerged.

Retail in a Lean World

Shifts in the structure of capital since the 1970s have been hard to miss. While countless authors have described their features, Mike Davis provides an interpretation built explicitly on the regulation framework: "What then *did* occur in the 1970s . . . was

7. In 1942 it achieved the 40-hour, five-day week; in 1949 company-sponsored health insurance; in 1953 a pension plan; in 1956, after a thirteen-day strike, a minimum $41 weekly wage, rising to $52 by 1962, as well as a nondiscrimination clause; in 1963 it won a 37.5-hour week for full-time employees; and in 1972, after an eight-day strike, dental and optical benefits (Local 1-S internal document).

the emergence of a new, embryonic regime of accumulation that might be called *overconsumptionism* . . . an increasing political subsidization of a sub-bourgeois, *mass* layer of managers, professionals, new entrepreneurs and rentiers who, faced with rapidly declining organization among the working poor and minorities during the 1970s, have been overwhelmingly successful in profiting from both inflation and expanded state expenditure" (1999, 211, emphasis in original). The flipside to the growth of professionals has been the dismantling of unionized industry and the explosion of low-wage services. Lichtenstein (2006, 2009) and Charles Fishman (2006) argue that Walmart has profited most from these trends while pushing aside many full-line department and independent stores. But pulled along in its tow have been myriad other chains. Some, such as Target and Costco, modified minor aspects of Walmart's model, while others, such as Toys "R" Us and Home Depot, applied analogous techniques to dominate specific product markets, earning the moniker "category killers" (Spector 2005).[8] Grocery firms, under competition from Walmart and other supercenters, have also undergone renewed concentration and conflict (Hurd 2008). Yet regardless of market niche, the biggest losers have been independent stores. Tables 2.1 and 2.2 provide industry-level overviews of these trends.

FOR TRADITIONAL DEPARTMENT stores, the growth of discounters and category killers has meant decline. Table 2.1 shows their slide in absolute and relative sales, but this is better illustrated by the history of Macy's. From its founding in 1858 members of R. H. Macy's

---

8. Toys 'R' Us, founded in 1957, predates Walmart; Robert Spector (2005) argues that it in fact provided the template copied by many other discounters and category killers.

TABLE 2.1

U.S. retail sales by NAICS subsector, 1992–2011

Retail subsector	1992		2011	
	Sales ($)	%	Sales ($)	%
Retail sales, total (in millions)	1,811,237	100.0	4,136,352	100.0
Motor vehicle and parts dealers	418,393	23.1	819,929	19.8
Furniture and home furnishings stores	52,336	2.9	90,073	2.2
Electronics and appliance stores	42,631	2.4	101,455	2.5
Building material and garden equipment dealers	130,989	7.2	279,068	6.7
Food and beverage stores	370,513	20.5	612,012	14.8
Health and personal care stores	89,705	5.0	272,073	6.6
Gasoline stations	156,324	8.6	529,093	12.8
Clothing and clothing access stores	120,103	6.6	229,312	5.5
Sporting goods, hobby, book, and music stores	49,026	2.7	82,392	2.0
General merchandise stores	247,876	13.7	630,256	15.2
Department stores	*181,255*	*10.0*	*188,476*	*4.6*
Full-line department stores	*87,384*	*4.8*	*66,358*	*1.6*
Discount department stores	*93,871*	*5.2*	*122,118*	*3.0*
Warehouse clubs and supercenters	*40,025*	*2.2*	*390,587*	*9.4*
All other general merchandise stores	*30,762*	*1.7*	*54,340*	*1.3*
Miscellaneous store retailers	54,840	3.0	111,977	2.7
Non-store retailers	78,501	4.3	378,712	9.2

Source: U.S. Census, Annual Retail Trade Survey, http://www.census.gov/retail/marts/www/timeseries.html.

family, and then that of the Straus brothers, held controlling shares until 1986, when Edward Finkelstein, the CEO, led a leveraged buyout (Barmash 1989). After a deep recession, the company filed for bankruptcy in 1993 and a year later was bought out by

TABLE 2.2

Four-firm concentration ratios by retail subsector, 1992–2007[a]

Retail subsector	Four-firm sales Concentration Ratios	
	1992	2007
Retail total	6.8	12.3
Motor vehicles and parts dealers	1.5	4.8
Furniture and home furnishings stores	9.7	13.9
Electronics and appliances stores		46.3
Building materials and garden dealers	16	40.6
Food and beverage stores	15.4	27.7
Eating and drinking places	7.9	N/A
Health and personal care stores	24.7	54.4
Gasoline stations	7.2	10.1
Clothing and clothing accessories stores	17.9	18.6
General merchandise stores	47.3	73.2
Miscellaneous retailers	5.4	21.8
Nonstore retailers		16.1
Sporting goods, hobby, music, books		23.8

Source: U.S. Economic Census 1992, 2007, http://www.census.gov/prod/www/economic_census.html.

[a] Prior to 1997, the U.S. Census Bureau used the Standard Industry Classification system (SIC), but then it switched to the North American Industry Classification System (NAICS), which divides the overall retail sector into twelve rather than nine subsectors. The census's Annual Retail Trade Survey has harmonized earlier data with the NAICS back to 1992, but the larger, cross-industrial economic census has not—hence the inclusion of more subsector categories in table 2.2 for 2007 (figures for 1992 are complete, but could not be disaggregated into later component subsectors).

Federated Department Stores (a national holding company). In 2005, Federated merged with May Department Stores (another holding company), renamed itself Macy's, Inc. and became the largest chain of full-line stores in the United States (National Retail

Federation 2013). Former regional nameplates, such as Filene's, Marshall Field's, and others, were rebranded as Macy's between 2003 and 2006. Bloomingdale's, now an upscale division of Macy's, was the sole exception. This example displays the general pattern of full-line stores, in their decline, undergoing rapid concentration that yielded a small number of large corporations: Macy's, Inc., Kohl's, Sears Holdings (now merged with Kmart), and J.C. Penney. Up-market chains, such as Neiman Marcus and Nordstrom's, remain, but these account for only small portions of department store and overall sales (ibid.).

SINCE 1980, THE RETAIL WORKFORCE has grown from 10.2 to 15.1 million individuals, while their real wages have fallen by 11 percent (to $14.02) and their average weekly hours, since 1972, by almost 14 percent (to 30.2) (U.S. Bureau of Labor Statistics 2014a). How do these trends connect to those of ownership and concentration? Walmart, again, is at the center of the story.

"The Wal-Mart shop floor," Adams asserts, is "the epitomous workplace of its respective epoch" (2006, 216). The firm's selling process is not a wholesale reinvention but "the perfection of the rule" identified as the key to discounters' success: "lower price markups, higher merchandise turnover, [and] almost total self-service" (214). At the same time, Walmart's centralized control, aided by real-time data flow from stores to headquarters, allows it to stress out store managers in a never-ending competition to keep staffing levels—and thus labor costs—down (Rosen 2006, 244). These individuals, who often work upwards of sixty hours a week, are held responsible for sales growth and relative wage costs, with large portions of their salaries derived from "bonuses" for meeting such goals.

Walmart's dominance has engendered a truly lean world for U.S. retail workers. Its presence in communities across the country has been associated with the decline of many independent shops, thus decreasing the scope for nonbureaucratized, small-scale employment (Fishman 2006; Lichtenstein 2009, 202–9). Its "everyday low prices" have also forced other retailers to imitate its cost structure and practices, which include "flexible" scheduling that matches staffing levels as tightly as possible to customer flow (Henly, Shaefer, and Waxman 2006; Lambert 2008). Chapters 3 and 4 provide in-depth examinations of similar dynamics at Target contrasted with the persistence of a semiskilled but increasingly precarious model at Macy's. In chapter 5 I consider the intersection of these practices with wider changes in the U.S. economy and workforce under neoliberalism.

IN 1983, ALMOST 11 PERCENT of retail workers were union members. By 2013, this had shrunk to 4.6 percent—below the 5 percent threshold at which unions have essentially zero influence (Lerner 2011). As table 2.3 shows, the largest concentration of members and the highest union density still lie in groceries. The next largest is in department stores, followed by drug stores. But department store unionization is so low as to be almost negligible, and density in the grocery sector has been halved since 1983. To explain the latter, Richard Hurd (2008) points to the continued regional focus of UFCW's collective bargaining in the context of increasingly national and international ownership. Unionism among vending machine operators has been completely wiped out since 2000, while in all other sectors it is at or below 5 percent.

For retail workers that are in unions, membership still makes a difference. In 2000, full-time unionized workers had median weekly earnings of $678, as opposed to $603 for their nonunion counterparts (in 2013 dollars). However, by 2013 both groups' real wages had atrophied to $622 and $601, respectively (U.S. Bureau of Labor Statistics 2014b). Lowered differentials present obvious challenges to future organizing, since unions have fewer advantages to point to.

TABLE 2.3

Union membership and density in selected retail subsectors, 1983 and 2013

	1983		2013	
	Members	Density	Members	Density
Lumber and building materials stores	25,829	7.4	13,082	1.5
Department stores[a]	145,744	7.4	52,255	2.4
Grocery stores	682,497	31.1	424,928	15.4
Motor vehicle dealers	48,491	6.5	24,135	2.0
Gasoline service stations	4,994	1.1	5,094	1.1
Apparel and accessory stores, excluding Shoe	23,588	3.6	6,355	0.7
Furniture and home furnishings stores	9,557	3.1	5,307	1.2
Household appliance, TV, and radio stores	2,729	1.1	14,771	2.8
Drug stores	33,665	7.2	38,722	4.7
Sporting goods, bicycles, and hobby stores	3,066	1.8	7,930	1.9
Liquor stores	9,489	8.1	6,460	5.3
Vending machine operators	10,426	18.6	0	0.0
Retail sector total	1,085,064	10.7	751,832	4.6

Source: Hirsch and Macpherson 2014.

[a] Includes discount stores and supercenters.

When it comes to organizing, "Wal-Mart is the 800-pound gorilla in the discussion" (Moody 2007, 233). As the largest private employer in the country, it is the obvious target for a broad-based renewal of the U.S. labor movement. Since the early 1990s, the UFCW has pursued several small-scale efforts, mainly with the goal of defending existing contracts with grocery chains. Lichtenstein (2009, 136) believes such a strategy "could never win" because of

Walmart's systematic union-prevention tactics. As demonstrated in two short-lived cases of successful organizing, one in 2000 of meat cutters in a Texas supercenter and the other in 2004 of an entire store in Quebec, the company has shown its ability to "cauterize the wound" by closing unionized stores or discontinuing entire departments, such as meat cutting (137). Given the low sunk costs of individual stores and the immense resources of most big-box firms, similar tactics are likely to be used against other small-scale campaigns, such as by Target after the failed Valley Stream drive (Becker 2014).

In 2004, after a disastrous strike and lockout among southern California grocers and a failed Las Vegas organizing drive, the UFCW refocused its efforts on a national Walmart campaign (Milkman 2004–5). These burst into view in 2012 with the arrival of the Organization United for Respect at Walmart (OUR Walmart), a nonunion worker association supported by the UFCW. Since then, OUR Walmart has led repeated one-day strikes and protests against its namesake. On "Black Friday," 2014, protests at nearly 1,500 of the company's U.S. stores highlighted its poverty-level wages and demanded workers' right to organize. These actions have also been linked to similar organizing by nonunion groups along Walmart's supply chain: Warehouse Workers United at the Greater Los Angeles and Warehouse Workers for Justice at the Greater Chicago distribution hubs (Slaughter 2012). As yet, these have not yielded union recognition or contracts, but they are widely credited with Walmart's move to upgrade maternal leave policy and its promise to raise entry-level wages to $10 by 2016 (DePillis 2014; Tabuchi 2015).

OUR Walmart, however, did not emerge from ether. Prior to 2012, a series of smaller campaigns informed its development. One was New York's Retail Action Project (RAP), initiated by the

RWDSU and a local community organization in 2005 to serve New York City retail workers. RAP has led successful campaigns against low-road retailers, including those for unionization and large back-wage settlements for workers at three clothing stores (Ikeler 2014). Other precursors include the International Longshore and Warehouse Union (ILWU)'s organization of nearly seven hundred Rite Aid distribution workers in 2008, key ingredients of which were coordination with the UFCW, SEIU, and Teamsters (Brown 2011). Less successful efforts also include the UFCW's "Wake Up Walmart" and Change to Win's "Cure CVS" campaigns. Both were largely air wars waged to turn public opinion against each company, but neither yielded tangible results.

These examples highlight the potential and challenges of retail organizing in twenty-first-century America. Faced with steady decline driven by the growth of big-box firms that deploy sophisticated union-prevention tactics, unions and worker centers have had to develop what Marshall Ganz (2009) calls "strategic capacity": going beyond legalistic procedures to challenge existing power structures. Such strategies, however, must connect with workers' consciousness and their day-to-day experience in order to have a chance at success. The goal of this narrative has been to show how the present conditions of U.S. retail workers are not simply the result of objective market conditions but are instead largely the outcome of historical contests between employers and workers against an evolving political and economic landscape. The next two chapters detail the divergent work processes used by different retailers, while chapter 5 shows how neoliberal changes are favoring one model over the other, engendering a regime of contingent control.

3

The Not-So-Hidden Abode

WORK ORGANIZATION AT
MACY'S AND TARGET

How are department stores organized today? Are they anything like the "palaces of consumption" of the 1920s or middle-market Sears of the 1950s? Or have they all been "Walmartized" around self-service, computerization, and short-staffing? These questions are less opaque than they might be for manufacturing—what Marx called the "hidden abode of production" ([1867] 1976, 279)—since retail plays out in semipublic spaces. We may think we understand what salespersons do, but our casual observations as customers provide only glimpses into their jobs and the overall processes they serve. In this chapter, I delve below the level of appearances to examine the organization of selling at Macy's and Target. I draw on the experiences of seventy-five workers to compare how the two firms divide their workforces, what salespersons and their nonselling colleagues do, how much they work together, and how much they control their effort.

The driving issue behind this is skill: whether work processes require salespersons to apply complex techniques and knowledge or follow rote procedures dictated by management. Task complexity and autonomy, as defined by labor process theorists, thus are central to this analysis. But service work also involves an interpersonal, emotional dimension, unlike noninteractive jobs.

Complexity and autonomy therefore play out on different terrain from the material interface of goods production. This chapter pays special attention to the structure of the emotional labor process and develops holistic depictions of it at Macy's and Target. Macy's I found used an eroded craft system: "eroded" with regard to its early twentieth-century predecessor and "craft" with regard to its specialized and relatively skilled sales style. With minor variations, this held for union and nonunion stores alike. Target, by contrast, used what I call service Toyotism: much like Japanese automakers and their emulators in the United States, it organized work in a collectivized, flexible fashion based on just-in-time delivery and management-sponsored "teamwork."

Division of Labor

Walking through a Macy's store, you pass by large areas of similar products—shoes, fragrances, jeans, handbags—often subdivided by brand. You may feel that certain areas are meant for you and others for those younger, older, or of a different gender. This is by design. Macy's arranges its departments by product, brand, and the target demographics of shoppers. Most sell apparel, with a minority dealing in jewelry, furniture, or household appliances. In the stores I studied, staffing varied with price and product. In men's suits, for example, "there are five or six tailors and about fifteen to twenty salespeople" and "the whole suit floor works on commission," said a salesman employed at Macy's for three years. In lower-priced departments, such as women's juniors, "there will be just a bunch of associates depending on how busy we are," none of whom earned commission (one-year saleswoman). Those in branded departments were often paid in part by their brand vendors. A one-year saleswoman stated that while "Macy's is my supervisor, we work with our vendor to produce the floor and make sure we sell the clothes." A two-year lingerie saleswoman described her store as "almost a bunch of different stores." Price and product were thus one axis along which labor was divided.

But there were other axes, horizontal and vertical. Within each department, "specialists" were distinguished from "associates" and "support staff." A storewide boundary separated these, in turn, from receiving and stock workers. Specialists "specialize in what they do but are not managers over the department" (four-year salesman). They maintained an overview of sales and displays for a given brand or section, delegating some tasks, but did not hire, fire, or set others' schedules. According to a five-year specialist, her job consisted in "more tasks but not really more money!" than associates, who were the largest group. Aside from advising customers, associates sorted and returned items, cleaned their areas, and rang up purchases. There were no dedicated cashiers. "Macy's doesn't have no cashiers," stated a two-year saleswoman. An eighteen-year saleswoman noted, "That has changed. When I came we had exit registers—the salespeople sold and the cashiers cashed." Support staff interacted less with customers and performed no register duties. "All I do is move around the merchandise and make sure everything is in order," said a one-year support worker. Another described her role as "censoring the merchandise, sizing the floor, and when we have new material, I make sure it's ready for restock." Merchandisers were a more elusive group. "I'm all merchandising," said one. "I don't deal with customers, I don't deal with sales, I just deal with set-up." Although some were employed by Macy's, many, like this woman, worked for outside subcontractors.

Vertical divisions involved the layers of management. At the floor level, managers were split between operations and sales, the first of which dealt with "all the stock, merchandising and filling" and the second of which "is just for the sales force, the salespeople and customer-related issues" (eighteen-year saleswoman). At the top of the pyramid was the general store manager, followed by sales floor managers, then sales group managers, "then that group manager has several managers running different departments." Most workers felt there were many managers. "On my floor," stated a salesman in a branded youth section, "there is one full-time manager and two part-time managers. There is a manager that works with customers which is apart from the group ones and then there is a manager on top of the managers for men's."

Gender and age also divided Macy's workforce. A one-year specialist in her early twenties echoed the views of others: "I would say more women work in the women's department and more men work in the men's department. The fifth floor has more older people because—I don't want to call it 'old people clothing' but it's more conservative." Two salespersons who worked in off-gender departments—a woman in men's suits and a man in women's juniors—were conscious of their outlier status. "Sometimes I'm standing with a colleague," the saleswoman related, "and a customer will come up and [it's like] I don't exist because it's a man thing." To the salesman, "it's like you're always under pressure because you're the only male, so you've got to show sales, you've got to show that you belong here."

Target stores offered a wider array of products than Macy's but fewer varieties of any one. Function, rather than brand, was the guiding principle. Stores had four broad departments— "hardlines," "softlines," pharmacy, and food—subdivided into roughly twenty specific areas, including sporting goods, stationery, women's wear, and frozen food, among others. Labor was divided not only among these departments but along the in-store supply chain: from backroom (receiving and stock) to in-stock to sales floor to front lanes (cash registers) and finally, to special services (customer returns, product questions, and shopping carts). There was also an in-store café, typically a Pizza Hut and a Starbuck's, the Team Member Services Center (human resources), and Asset Protection (security). All workers, regardless of department, were "team members." A one-year backroom worker outlined this structure:

> You have the sales-floor team members, they keep the store brand and organized. . . . You have the cashiers of course; then you have the in-stock team members, [who take] the stuff we pull from upstairs and load onto flats or tubs and push them out. Then they also have different departments like softlines, that's all clothes, hardlines, [where] you have team members in charge of toys, kitchen stuff, and electronics. They train you so that in case they are short in one area they could call on you and you could fill that position.

Each department was a team with its own internal hierarchy. Team members were the lowest and most numerous on this ladder and were often moved around by managers, or moved on their own to gain more hours. As a three-year cashier put it, "Everybody is cross-trained, that way if another department needs help they can take one of the cashiers." Just above team members were specialists, nonsupervisory employees who "use their individual expertise to increase performance in a specific area of the store such as Electronics or Jewelry" (Target Corporation 2008, 17). Specialists were candidates for the first rung of supervision (team leader, or TL), were guaranteed forty weekly hours (unlike team members), but earned little more—one woman reported a twenty-five-cent raise upon her promotion to specialist.

Every team had one leader and one or two specialists. "The supervisor is the team leader," said a one-year stock worker, "and then the boss is the higher rank. The supervisor gives the report to the boss, so the boss doesn't normally work with us—it's the team lead[er]." The "boss" was the executive team leader (ETL). These individuals performed few if any frontline tasks, were "responsible for a specific area of store operations such as Logistics (stocking), Guest Experience, Hardlines, [or] Softlines," and were paid annual salaries rather than hourly wages (Target Corporation 2008, 17). Above ETLs was a single "store team leader" (STL), whom workers at one store knew as Mike: "He is in charge of everything. He sometimes makes stupid decisions but he is in charge of everything" (one-year backroom worker).

Within these divisions, Target allocated workers by gender. As at Macy's, salespersons often found themselves in departments geared toward same-sex customers. A first-year softlines saleswoman remarked that where she worked, "it's mostly women; there is three dudes out of thirty or forty [employees]." "I didn't ask for this section," she continued. "I wanted to be in electronics, but in my interview they just said they are going to put me in softlines, 'do you mind?'" A one-year team member at a different store observed that "softlines is mostly all girls and electronics is mostly guys." Nevertheless, salespersons were relatively mixed in comparison with stock workers and cashiers. "If you go to the checkout lanes," said a four-year salesman, "you will see a majority of girls there. Guys go for backroom, logistics. . . . If you look at guest services, it's mostly girls." Starting pay in the male-dominated backroom and electronics departments was a dollar more than that for cashiers and nonelectronics salespersons.

Similarities did exist between Macy's and Target. Both distributed workers along an in-store supply chain and both had overlapping positions—specialists, sales associates and sales-floor team members, sales support and in-stock. One clear difference, however, was that only Target had centralized checkout and dedicated cashiers—both absent at Macy's. A second difference was flexibility: Target workers rotated among departments and along the supply chain, while workers at unionized Macy's did so only when promoted or transferred. But nonunion Macy's more closely resembled Target on this score: "What we have is home sections," said a first-year saleswoman there, "but you can pick up shifts throughout the whole store."

Tasks and Routines

> As the years went by, the salesperson does everything. We used to have stock people, now I think there's one stock person for the whole floor. You do everything, you are a glorified stock person. (Thirty-one-year Macy's salesman)

> I mean it's a simple job, it's not like you have to think a lot. Sometimes you think about "what should I put here?" but you don't have to go in-depth about what you know. It's kind of relaxing. (One-year Target salesman)

When I spoke with Macy's and Target workers I asked them to describe their daily routines. From their descriptions two pictures emerged: eroded craft selling at Macy's and routinized flexibility, or service Toyotism, at Target. Macy's workers, rather than performing highly subdivided and simplified tasks, were required to do more and more, becoming all-around workers. Target workers performed detailed tasks that were considerably simpler, yet few were rigidly bound to any particular role. Here I depict these differing routines in the words of those who lived them.

Macy's salespersons did much more than sell. They continually performed multiple upkeep tasks within their departments. One four-year saleswoman stated, "We come in, open up the registers, see if there are any rods on the floor or clothes that need to be put back in any of the areas that they [managers] put us in for the day. We put the merchandise out on the floor, making sure that the area is clean for when we open up." Another four-year saleswoman noted the importance of making sure "your wrap stand [register] is clean, that you have all the basic materials you need, such as receipt paper, labels to label the items with, your bags—it's very important to have your bags and no messy wrap stand, some scissors." Such maintenance work extended throughout the day and was mainly the concern of support staff during heavy shopping hours. "Usually we have more people closing and opening," said a one-year specialist, "because it takes a lot of work to get the store back in order after everybody has finished their shopping." Intervening periods were filled more with customer interaction.

Salespersons needed knowledge and charisma to interact with customers and generate sales. To this end, Macy's had devised the "MAGIC" selling method, in which it trained personnel twice a year. MAGIC was an acronym:

> The M stands for "meet and make a connection": you meet a customer and you make a connection with them, compliment them on their sweater. . . . The A is for "asking questions"—the key is that you are supposed to ask open-ended questions. . . . The G is "give advice": you can give advice like, "oh, are you going to a wedding? Then you should wear this." The I is for "inspire to buy": so you could say, "oh, you're going to a wedding, but how about for dancing?" . . . Then the C is for "celebrate the purchase": after you ring them up you give them a reason to come back, make them smile. (Two-year shoe salesman)

In practice, many salespersons used their own interpersonal style and acquired product knowledge rather than this procedure. The same two-year salesman stated, "I sort of use MAGIC, but really

I'm more of a comedy person, so I try to stand out by my attitude and my luck." A one-year specialist found that "with the MAGIC classes they train you, but I just learned to be real patient and observant with customers because you can't come up to every customer the same way." And an eleven-year saleswoman believed "it's pretty much about being yourself, if you enjoy talking and selling. . . . We all do our own thing." MAGIC, she noted, was just another managerial fad: "A few years ago the word was "outstanding" or something—it's always something."

Salespersons often had to speak knowledgeably about products to customers, and this increased with products' price. In men's suits, for example, "you have to demonstrate your product knowledge. . . . You are supposed to garner clients who you can call up and tell when there is a sale" (two-year saleswoman). A three-year salesman from the same department said, "I didn't know anything about suits when I first started"; he "learn[ed] everything just by talking to other sales associates and managers" and could describe in great detail contemporary men's fashions:

> What's popular right now is two buttons, and two slits in the back, sometimes there is one in the middle and that is not as popular now. Then they have the peak lapels which are coming back in which you would find mostly in the '50s and '60s and '70s. That's coming back because it looks better on the slim suits. And then there are three-button suits, that's not as popular, but still kind of with the Jewish community. Three-button suits were more in style ten, fifteen years ago, now everything is two buttons.

Men's suits and other high-value departments were commission-based: salespersons earned a percentage of every sale. In noncommissioned departments, which were the majority, specialists were expected "to know more about the merchandise" than associates (one-year specialist). But many noncommissioned salespersons also emphasized their knowledge. "You got to know the product on each floor and in your area and in the building. On my floor it's good to know the jeans so you can inform the customer on how the fit is. . . . We know our product—we have to know" (eleven-year saleswoman, non-commissioned).

The complexity of selling combined with maintenance tasks and sales quotas (discussed below) created tension at Macy's. A five-year specialist argued that "because of these demands what actually happens is that the people who don't make [customers] happy stay by the register and have most of the contacts with customers, whereas you have to recover the mess that is left." Another described "associates just get[ting] hired, get[ting] thrown out in the field and spend[ing] all day at the registers" (ten-year specialist). Because quotas were attained only by ringing up purchases, those who lacked experience sometimes tried to circumvent the process. This was made easier by limited equipment: "In one department I have two registers but six persons working, each with a $1,000 goal. How could, in the same working hours, six people make the same target?" asked a four-year specialist.

Competing demands made for anything but a simple routine. "There's only a certain number of things you have to do, but collectively it's a lot of work," said a two-year support worker. A four-year saleswoman's breathless response when I asked if management required multitasking was indicative:

> Do they? Oh my God, we do! How can I say it? We answer the phone, we register the person out, we go back to the floor, look for the item, we retake the item, pack the item, we also have to check the fitting rooms and put the clothes back, we also have to maintain the floors, right? You also have to open up credit, right? And then sometimes you have to

go check the stockroom as well and get—what else do we have to do? That's basically it. That's a lot of multitasking and we also have to order.

Most salespersons described similar workloads. Against the backdrop of sales quotas and staffing declines, this provided strong evidence of speedup. But selling remained individualized: each salesperson was responsible for seeking out customers, advising them, and closing purchases. To do this they deployed considerable knowledge in some cases and a personalized pitch in most. Thus despite the removal of countertops and the rise of branding and advertising since the mid-twentieth century, Macy's sales process still retained craft characteristics, though eroded from its prewar predecessor. This erosion had gone much further at Target.

> The routine is you come in and if there is re-shop, you put it where it is supposed to be, you take it to the back. Then you get back to your zone and you zone it, that means you push everything forward and make it look neat and clean, that's basically what we do. And help customers. (First-year Target salesman, electronics)

Selling was beyond the reach of any individual at Target. Workers performed only pieces of the process, with much persuasion effected by the store's standardized displays and external advertising. The flow of goods through the store—and partial backflow from returned, misplaced, and damaged items—was managed by an integrated computer system that connected team members and supervisors through an assortment of handheld and stationary devices. The tasks of frontline workers consisted in maintaining aspects of this flow and creating a positive, helpful environment.

"My position is a backroom team member," said a one-year employee in his twenties. "We pull the merchandise that people buy. It is a [machine] generated system that works through the cashiers, so every hour in the backroom different categories drop of the merchandise people buy so we pull the items and get them onto the shelves with a sense of urgency." After receiving crews unloaded merchandise from overnight delivery trucks, back-room workers were the next to handle products on their journey through the store. Their title indicated what another such worker stated: "We don't really have interactions with customers. If any-thing, the team members downstairs [on the sales floor] will call us upstairs if the customer needs something." Backroom workers performed back-stocking and pulling. "Back-stocking is anything that comes into the store, we have to make sure that the stuff is in the system" (first-year team member). Pulling, according to a first-year backroom worker, took place "every hour. Whatever is needed on the sales floor which registers to the PDA [personal data assis-tant], we pull it and load them up and send it downstairs accord-ing to which floor they go to, so we separate them according to their floor or the department." In addition, they sorted and moved some items to a section called "chargeback"—"where everything goes that doesn't have a barcode or is damaged" (first-year back-room worker). "They waste a lot," he continued, "like thousands of dollars of food and furniture and toys every day."

The next workers to handle merchandise were those on the in-stock team. They picked up carts of goods filled by backroom workers, brought these out, and placed them on shelves. A four-year salesman and former in-stock worker described these tasks succinctly:

You come in, you scan items that are out of stock, if it is empty then you scan the shelf label and—it's a system-generated thing—if it's up-stairs [in the backroom] they will send it down; if it's not, the scanner will order it from the headquarters and they will send it in. So it's basically replenishment and we pack it out on the shelves.

Unlike backroom workers, in-stock workers occasionally interacted with customers and were expected to assist them. "Guests come up to me and say 'oh I need this, I need to buy that,'" said a one-year in-stock worker and former salesman, but "not as often as when I was on the sales floor."

Salespersons performed "zoning," "re-shop," and customer service. The first of these was "straightening and cleaning each department . . . so that each item is in its proper place" (Target Corporation 2008, 64). "Proper place" was stipulated in planograms (display blueprints) distributed from corporate headquarters (ibid.). Re-shop was "when you take the items and put them back on the shelf or, if it is damaged, move it from the floor to the backroom" (two-year saleswoman). The following description from a first-year saleswoman illustrated the interplay of re-shop and zoning tasks in a "softlines" department:

> Re-shop is like if you are in the fitting room, everything that people try on and don't want? We put it on a T-rack. By the end of the night, all of the clothes that the people tried on during the day have to be back on the floor. Zoning is making everything small, medium, large, proper areas. Pickups is multitasking—we make sure there is nothing on the floor, no re-shop in the fitting room. If there is re-shop in the fitting room they're going to run after us like, Do your re-shop! Do your re-shop! Hurry up, we have to leave by eleven o'clock!

Salespersons used the PDA to communicate with backroom workers and access the store's inventory. "The PDA is the biggest thing because we use it so much," said a one-year softlines specialist. "Basically it is the whole store in one little machine." "For me," she continued, "I need it every day, all the time; a regular salesperson wouldn't need it that much."

Customer service punctuated zoning and re-shop tasks. "We zone, zone, zone," said a four-year saleswoman, "and they want us to be nice and gracious to everybody who comes in." Target's service motto was "Fast, Fun, and Friendly," and its signature pitch, "Can I help you find something?" Salespersons and in-stock workers were coached to ask this of all customers ("guests") who came within ten feet of them and to interrupt noninteractive tasks to do so. A one-year saleswoman described this as "being readily available to guests any time they need something. A couple of days ago I was working in pets and seasonal, but on my way to somewhere else I got stopped by three different guests and had to call backroom for three different items. . . . Our motto is fast, fun, and friendly. And just be there." But customer interaction was not always so fast, fun, or friendly. A one-year salesman and recent West African immigrant discussed his difficulties:

> Sometimes I tell the guests "go to this aisle" and then they come back and say "I can't find it," so I have to go and look for it myself. Sometimes they have personal problems and they bring that into the store and get some sort of confusion. Others have a language barrier, they speak Spanish, I don't speak Spanish. If there is no team member around to help me I become an ashtray, let me put it that way.

And a one-year softlines specialist found the phrase "Can I help you find something?" "so annoying"

> because they literally have us, every five minutes asking every single customer "Can I help you find something?" Mind you, that customer has probably been asked "Can I help you find something?" twenty times that day, so it's annoying to the customer and annoying to us because we can't get done what we have to get done.

Target's signature question nonetheless reflected the type of knowledge it expected of salespersons. In contrast to Macy's, where salespersons had to know about product features to advise and make sales, their Target peers simply needed to know where things were. "Training took me two weeks," said a first-year saleswoman, "but after the first week I was already pretty much familiar with everything, because they are always willing to help you out." Only the electronics and frozen food departments required some product knowledge. "Electronics," said a two-year salesman, "urges us to push more guest experience because we get scored on attachments [sold]" such as speakers and HDMI cables. A four-year stationery saleswoman confirmed that "in electronics they have to be knowledgeable, but not for me—no knowledge is necessary."

The last group to handle products and customers on their path through the store were cashiers. Their jobs were the most routinized at Target. "It's nothing too complicated," said a first-year male cashier. "It's basically the same thing over and over again." "It's not that difficult of a job," stated a first-year female cashier. "The register practically runs itself—you just have to read the stream." A two-year cashier compared her current role unfavorably with her previous one as a café server:

> Yeah, I hate it. Because you just sit there all day and just beep, beep, beep. It's supposed to move fast but some people, when they look at the total are like, "oh wow, can you take that back?" So you have to stop and scroll and look at what they have, and some of the stuff doesn't have a name on it so you don't know exactly what it is.

Cashiers' work followed the dictates of the register. After scanning each item's barcode, the machine tallied the bill, added tax, registered inventory changes, and indicated whether an ID check was necessary. Customers, however, were unpredictable. "We are here to help them," said the first-year male cashier, "but sometimes they are really crazy, that is one thing I hate about [being a] cashier." The first-year female cashier found customers "the hardest part. It's not the employees or the employer, but the customers." The speed at which cashiers completed transactions—from the first item scanned to final payment—was timed and recorded. Low speeds could lead to poor reviews by team leaders, which could adversely affect pay, hours, and ultimately job security.

Selling at Macy's was an individual effort that required salespersons to use intuition, persuasion, and knowledge to guide interactions toward purchase. Their emotional labor approached the "deep acting" once performed by flight attendants (Hochschild 1983) and insurance salespeople (Leidner 1993). At Target, selling was simplified. Salespersons aided customers in locating products and prices but rarely advised them about product features or brands. Stakes were also lower than at Macy's, since purchases were not recorded for individual salespersons. They were, however, recorded for cashiers, who were judged not on the content or quality of their service but on their speed. The emotional labor of Target salespersons and cashiers thus closely resembled the "surface acting" of fast-food servers (Leidner 1993). Finally, the flow of tasks at Macy's was less dictated by computer systems than at Target, where almost every move of every worker was guided, recorded, or directed by some electronic device.

Collectivization

Collectivization is the degree to which workers complete tasks cooperatively. Though it is not an intrinsic part of skill, its growth often accompanies the simplification of tasks and enables greater productivity. Marx identified this for manufacturing in the nineteenth century: "The labour of each, as a part of the labour of all, may correspond to a distinct phase of the labour process; and as a result of the system of co-operation, the object of labour passes through the phases of the process more quickly" ([1867] 1976, 444). At Macy's we saw that selling was individualized. This often generated competition—the opposite of cooperation—among salespersons:

Q: Do the goals ever create competition among salespeople?

A: Oh yeah, they are always fighting over their goals. Like, "oh I need to ring them here" or "I'm supposed to ring." It's created a problem between associates. (Eight-year saleswoman)

Q: Does the goals system ever produce . . . ?

A: Tension? Yeah, every single day, it's very competitive. If you see a customer you want to run after them before someone else does because someone else will get the sale instead of you. (One-year saleswoman)

Within this competitive framework, however, workers sometimes had to cooperate to make a particular sale or raise the sales of the entire department (for which supervisors were held accountable). "If I am trying to sell a top to your dress," explained an eleven-year saleswoman, "and a customer wants the same material-wise and I'm not sure, then someone else can tell me whether the material is really a hundred percent cotton." Asked if she collaborated with colleagues to make sales, a four-year saleswoman replied, "Yes, especially with bra measuring. We see all the ladies!" And at times of high customer volume, some salespersons helped each other reach their goals: "If it's really busy, then we work things out and say, "I'll be on the register for this amount of time and then you can go on," because we all know that we have goals so we help each other. If I made my goal and one of my associates didn't, I would help them make theirs" (one-year specialist).

Macy's salespersons often received training from senior coworkers. After listing the register functions taught him by managers, a two-year salesman acknowledged that "every other function I basically learned with associates' help" and a four-year saleswoman considered her coworkers "family" because she had "worked with them for four and a half years and they teach me to do different things." Sales quotas strongly discouraged cooperation, for obvious reasons, but the expansion of maintenance duties worked in the opposite direction. A five-year specialist noted that she regularly helped her coworkers "fold their area if my area is clean." A two-year support worker found that her tasks consisted in "a lot of teamwork. If you are fixing a table, you have the right to ask your colleagues for help. There are also a lot of clearance trays, about five or six and you can't do all of them by yourself. If you are the only person you ask for help." And a four-year saleswoman affirmed that "even when Macy's doesn't have a supervisor on our floor we still join together and do what we have to do." Quotas provided an impetus to cooperate on maintenance, since an orderly department raised everyone's chances of selling: "I sell better if my house is in order," said an eight-year saleswoman.

But an impetus is not an actuality, as a five-year specialist noted: "The part-timers, they would just like to ring and make their goal and not clean up. But most of the full-timers they want to see the department clean." A four-year specialist also indicated that non-selling tasks were less valued by management:

> The time you are outside the register they call "unproductive hours," which means you are not selling, you are doing something that helps the sale but is called unproductive. Only the time you are ringing, that's

a "productive hour." So we have to ask the manager to give us "unproductive hours"; otherwise that will be a minus from our scorecard.

Negotiation over who would perform these unproductive functions created further friction, which, alongside goal attainment, remained unresolved. A two-year saleswoman felt that Macy's overall sales process was "individualistic ... it's a dog-eat-dog kind of world." Thus despite instances of cooperation, competition predominated. Target was a very different environment.

> We call it one team, one dream. Each department is one team, like softlines, electronics, health and beauty, but if health and beauty is not done and we are, then we go to help them, so everybody is just one team, all together. We help each other out all the time; everybody has to help each other out. (First-year Target saleswoman)

Maintenance work at Macy's was relatively collectivized within each department. But cooperation across departments was almost nonexistent, and service tasks were organized in a broadly competitive fashion. At Target these barriers to cooperation were nonexistent: not only did salespersons work together to complete departmental maintenance, but they also cooperated across departments to help others achieve these ends when staff were few or customers many. Sales quotas, as mentioned above, were tallied for the store as a whole rather than for individuals or even specific departments. Target's service tasks, in contrast to those at Macy's, were thus also collectivized. A common refrain from participants, reflecting a corporate motto, was that each store was "one team, one dream."

"Working together?" replied a one-year softlines specialist to a question about cooperation. "A good 90 percent of the time. The only time I would be by myself is if I'm the only one in the store, say from eight until nine, but mostly working together." A one-year in-stock worker from another store found that "there is no single day we move apart; we are always together." And a first-year salesman in the market section described the necessity of cooperation for completing re-shop and zoning tasks:

> Say me and another worker are in the dry market area and there are two sides so at the end of the night we know that side is yours, this side is mine, and if there is any re-shop it is for the whole section so we will put our carts together and get all the re-shop out. At night there is something we call wave zoning where you take this side, I take that side, and we just zone each aisle together. So yeah, we do work together a lot.

Although tasks were often delegated by team leaders to individual workers, completion of zoning and re-shop (for sales areas) or pulling and pushing (for backroom and in-stock) were group objectives. "Some days the workload is heavy," said a four-year salesman, "and if the manager doesn't know that you need help, you will be stuck and the manager will hold you accountable. So you have to cooperate." A first-year softlines saleswoman found that "the people who work in the morning—we depend on them because at night we depend on each other. The closing team, if we leave re-shop, the morning team has to do it, and if the morning team never does the re-shop then we have to do that. So we definitely depend on each other a lot." Even cashiers cooperated at times to overcome snags in the check-out process: "Whenever I need help and I go to any other girl or boy who is next to me they do help," stated a first-year cashier.

Target workers also cooperated across departments on maintenance and stocking duties as well as customer service and sales. "Sometimes when in-stock need help," said a first-year backroom worker, "we will take stuff from them and bring it upstairs. I take stuff downstairs myself sometimes from the freezer. Sometimes when my team comes in, people come upstairs from the sales floor and ask, ok, what do we got? What we need to push?" There was little permanent separation between backroom, in-stock, and some salespersons, who traded roles when necessary. A one-year backroom worker commented that "if it's very busy, then the manager may ask a team member from the sales floor to help us out." Cross-departmental cooperation also took place between salespersons and cashiers. "They always train you on the sales floor and on the cash register," said a first-year salesman, "because it gets really busy in the store and they sometimes call for back-up, so everyone knows how to work the register." And cross-training extended to different sales departments. "In my store we all got to know each other and we do everything," said another first-year saleswoman. "I will come on a shift," she continued, "'you're upstairs tonight'; I'll come on a shift, 'you're downstairs tonight.' OK, that's what I do, that's how it is." "So everybody is kind of cross-trained?" I asked a different first-year saleswoman. "Yeah," she answered, "I am in the market department but I am also cross-trained in chemicals where they sell cleaning supplies, I can get cross-trained in electronics, the clothes department. The whole thing is fast, fun, and friendly—everyone is always on the walkie [talkie], helping each other out."

In addition to computerized inventory, walkie-talkies enabled storewide cooperation. "We use the walk-talkies to communicate in the store," said a three-year salesman. "The only people who have their own separate walkies is Asset Protection, but everyone else, from the store manager down to the newest team member, can all speak to each other on the walkie."

Collectivization was a minor trend at Macy's. Workers there, whether union or nonunion, cooperated to train new colleagues, maintain their departments, and occasionally, such as when shopping was heavy, to mutually attain goals. But the general pattern was individualized competition. Not so at Target. Target had collectivized not only stocking and maintenance but selling and interaction as well, and this was aided in no small part by technology. Target's selling process was thus more capital-intensive than that of Macy's or similar full-line department stores. Technology, as Braverman (1974) argued, is rarely a neutral arbiter of workplace efficiency; it reflects social relations and, in a capitalist framework, often diminishes worker autonomy while increasing managerial control.

Control

Control and autonomy are more ambiguous than they may seem. To understand their meaning for a given work environment we need to conceptualize the labor process as a whole and then determine where and with what degrees of freedom frontline workers fit in. Modern retail is complex: from supplier to consumer, a variety of workers, including salespersons, execute myriad intermediary tasks. What and how much to buy, when to ship, when to stock, how to display, which customers to target, how much to charge—all of this is decided by management before workers ever set foot in the store. The bandwidth of decision making for twenty-first-century salespersons is thus narrower than for independent shopkeepers, the precapitalist benchmark against which Burawoy (1978) believes we should judge occupations.

And this depiction holds as much for Macy's as for Target. Concerning those decisions remaining to salespersons, the control/autonomy question reduces to these: To what extent are workers' inputs (attendance, maintenance activities, approaching customers, etc.) self- or other-directed? With what precision and consequences are workers' outputs (sales, cleanliness, etc.) measured by management? I found that while Macy's salespersons retained considerable autonomy over their inputs, their output was controlled in an ever-more rigid fashion. At Target, salespersons' inputs and outputs were closely watched by management, indicating lower autonomy for them than for their Macy's peers.

Most Macy's workers had some degree of freedom. A six-year specialist stated, "If I see [my manager] for five minutes during a shift, that could be a lot. They generally stay behind closed doors." A two-year support worker found that while in his first three months supervisors would direct him throughout the day, "now no one has to tell [me] anything." "We do our own thing," said a five-year specialist. "They [managers] tell us what to do, but if we don't feel like doing it we don't really do it."

Direct oversight, however, was not absent: "Sometimes you see them lurking when you're doing a sale; they're watching what you do to give you feedback" (two-year saleswoman). A one-year specialist described how managers discouraged socializing and returned workers to maintenance or selling tasks:

> When I started working there they were like, "oh, you're clumping" and I was like, "what is that"? Clumping is when people stand together and talk. But it's not clumping when you [managers] do it, when you stand together with an associate and talk, but when associates do it with each other it's clumping so I'm like, all right!

Others highlighted oversight by vendor representatives. "They are usually harder on me than the [Macy's] managers," said a second-year support worker. "Because they work for the brand, they need to make sure everything is good." Another support worker in a branded area believed "Macy's managers become like supervisors" for vendors, noting they would report to her vendor whenever she was late. And many nonunion Macy's workers believed their in-store security systems—guards, censors, and cameras—were directed more at them than at customers: "Security is watching," said a two-year saleswoman. "They watch us all the time; they watch us harder than they watch you guys [customers] on the camera."

Attendance and behavior were also monitored through a point system. "You get a point for being late, three points for calling out, and there are also behavioral write-ups. You need fifteen of them [points] to get a written warning. It's ridiculous," said an assistant manager at a unionized Macy's. Points were wiped clean every three months, which this supervisor attributed to union presence: "I have associates who come late every single day but nothing ever happens when you're in a union store." "Their union is pretty strong," he continued, "so it's almost impossible to get somebody fired unless they are sexually harassing or something." At nonunion stores this was not the case: "Oh no, we get fired for that," said a first-year saleswoman. "If you get zero points you get automatically fired."

Salespersons thus had some discretion over inputs, which increased with their seniority. Given the MAGIC sales method, this made sense: salespersons needed leeway to pursue customer wishes and inspire them to buy more. But if inputs were only loosely controlled, output was tightly monitored through Macy's quota system. At the start of my inquiry there were four basic measurements, which were reduced to three in early 2012. Combined with point deductions for lateness, absences, or "unruly" behavior (being out of dress code, arguing with coworkers, managers, or customers), these measures comprised each salesperson's weekly scorecard. Scorecards, which had one hundred possible points, were calculated "weekly, monthly and yearly, and all will add to your [annual] review" (four-year specialist). The four sales measurements were (1) total daily, weekly, etc. sales and whether they met the relevant quota; (2) average sales per hour, day, week, etc.; (3) the number of Macy's credit cards opened; and (4) (removed in 2012) the number of items sold per customer transaction (IPT). Sales goals were generated based on the store's sales that date the previous year "plus an incremental increase," according to Ken Bordieri, Local 1-S president:

> It depends on what shift you're working. If you're working on a Saturday your goal might be higher than on a Monday. If it's a busy day you will get a higher goal; if you're working the morning shift you will get a smaller goal compared to a later shift because later on in the day it'll pick up. And it depends how many hours you work, but the goal basically equals out between everybody working at the counter [department], so the counter also has one goal, which Macy's gives to us.

A four-year specialist, however, noted that in his department "one person on the same day might have a $1,500 goal, and the other person a $1,100 goal." Sales metrics were measured when salespersons rang up customers after logging in with a personal identification number.

Full-time salespersons were expected to open three and part-timers two Macy's credit cards per week; depending on department, the expected items per transaction were either two or three. When asked whether she thought sales quotas were realistic, a one-year specialist responded, "Sometimes they are, sometimes they aren't. I'm only at 15 percent of my goal for today and I've been here since 9:45" when it was currently one o'clock. Asked the same question, a first-year saleswoman replied, "Yes, but for the month of January it was really, really slow because nobody was shopping. And they were giving us these really high goals and nobody was making them. So they understand that there's not much you can do in that situation." If the goal for a given day was too high, echoed a five-year specialist, "then there is nothing you can do. You make it up on another day if you ring like 200 percent, which you can." Items later returned were deducted from salespersons' totals, which could retroactively affect goal attainment. That's why a one-year specialist's "manager says to ring about 130 percent of your goal to cater for the returns."

The impact of such metrics on workers' pay and job security was less at unionized Macy's stores than at their nonunion counterparts:

Q: Could someone be demoted or punished on the basis of these reviews?

A: No. In the nonunion stores, yes. That's one of the things that they were trying to push during the negotiations, that we should be able to demote someone who's not making their goals. (Eighteen-year saleswoman and shop steward)

Annual reviews impacted raises, but "even if you make the metrics you just get like five cents or ten cents; even when you are really good you only get fifteen cents," she continued. Promotion or transfer opportunities, however, were affected: "If your scorecard is not in the 70–100 point range," said a first-year saleswoman, "your chances of getting a promotion are very minimal because at the end of the day they use this scorecard system to promote you."

Salespersons' output was thus highly controlled. They could not determine how quotas were set and only certain aspects of whether they attained them. On a slow day quotas could be impossible to make, and even when they were met or exceeded, they could later be undone by customer returns. Little surprise then that many workers disliked this policy: "That goals system? It's a mess. They need to get rid of it. Nobody thinks about the customers, they only think about their goals" (two-year saleswoman).

With the exception of cashiers' checkout speeds, Target did not use individualized goals. But output was rigorously measured and inputs more closely directed than at Macy's. Here is the view of a first-year Target saleswoman who previously worked at a unionized Macy's:

> I pretty much did anything I wanted in Macy's, they didn't have strict guidelines. The only thing they were strict about was trying to get everybody to sign up for the Macy's card. Target is a little more strict, I guess since they are used to dealing with kids [younger workers], so they are on you making sure you're on time, on you for doing your work and stuff, so it's different.

In some respects, Target's work process corresponded to Aglietta's description of Fordism, discussed in chapter 2. But Target workers were not "fixed" to their jobs by inflexible machinery; instead, they rotated among standardized positions. This routinized flexibility fit closely with what analysts refer to as "lean production" (Moody 1997; Womack and Jones 2003), the "Japanese model" (Milkman 1991; Graham 1995), or Toyotism (Dohse, Jürgens and Malsch 1985). Target's sales process was therefore a form of service Toyotism.

What does this tell us about control? The minute subdivision of tasks and their coordination by computerized inventory systems provided evidence of what Edwards (1979) calls "technical control"—regulating worker behavior through machinery and the design of tasks. But Target's complex rules and procedures for almost every employee action—stricter and more comprehensive than Macy's—also provided evidence for Edwards's alternate model, "bureaucratic control." Together, these features engendered lower autonomy for Target's workers than for Macy's.

When I asked a three-year salesman whether there were rules for zoning, he replied, "Yes. You have to make sure that every item is in the right location—sometimes it's two faces, sometimes it's forward-facing, sometimes there are four items . . . and they should be forward facing." The design of displays and workers' attendant zoning and re-shop tasks were meticulously specified in "planograms" for each department. Another three-year salesman and former team leader described how he used these in his previous role:

> It's like a blueprint that gives you all the information you need to know. I would hand it out to my team members and basically my role as a team leader was just giving them the planograms and managing—like if one finished early I could have them help the next one and just get the whole job done throughout the night. And I had to walk around and identify any problems, anything that could be fixed.

Such meticulous prespecification minimized both frontline workers' and first-level supervisors' decision-making. As one four-year saleswoman put it, "You know what you have to do, you know what departments need and you just go to them, get whatever stuff you need from the back to the floor and when that's done you just start keeping the shelves neat for the next day. So that's pretty much the job right now, pretty routine. Nobody has to tell me, I already know." "You only make decisions for yourself," stated a first-year salesman, "if there is something—it's called 'flexing it'—where you just put it out because there is no more space; mainly sale items."

Standardization also extended to customer service: "Can I help you find something?" as the universal greeting for all customers, combined with the "fast, fun, and friendly" approach. Three pages of Target's employee handbook discussed the appropriate use of this greeting, including an instructive FAQ:

> Q: Do I have to specifically ask "Can I help you find something?" or can I use my own words?
>
> A: Think of "Can I help you find something?" as our service trademark. If guests hear team members consistently ask the same question, over time they will associate the exact phrase with Target, making it part of our brand. (Target Corporation 2008, 13)

Further Q and A's stipulated when it was appropriate and when not to ask, 'Can I help you find something?' the latter including "if a guest is distracted," when he or she "may be busy with kids, having a fun time with friends or on the phone" (ibid.). Fast, fun, and friendly was defined as "the 'personality' of the Target brand. It's more than being nice to each other and to guests. . . . It's how we bring the brand to life for our guests and fellow team members" (ibid., 8).

The only means of monitoring salespersons' compliance with these standards was through first-hand observation. "They have supervisors that watch you," said the four-year saleswoman quoted earlier, echoing a theme from Macy's: "You don't know they watch you but they watch you." A first-year saleswoman stated that "the team leads constantly walk the floor to see if we are on task and not loafing," and another from the same store repeated the opinion of others: "I believe they use the [in-store] cameras to watch how everybody is working. I mean they would always come out and say, 'hey, I see you on the camera doing this or doing that.'"

But for backroom, in-stock, and cashiers, output and compliance were measured quantitatively. "If you use the scanner," said a four-year former in-stock worker, "it tells them exactly what you do because you have to put your name and numbers in to start the scanner." Another one-year in-stock worker described the use of scorecards for each worker:

> Based on how fast you scan, how you fix rechecks and if you are able to come out a clean shift . . . you are 100 percent. If you get ten rechecks and you fix five, where are the rest of the five? That means you are going down. So every month they give us our score based on our scanning, how fast we scan and how we fix the rechecks, individually.

The speed and accuracy with which backroom workers pulled merchandise was similarly recorded:

> The cab [computer screen order] drops every hour on the hour and we have to pull all that merchandise in one hour, or as close as possible. If we go over then it turns up on the paperwork as red, which means we haven't pulled those items within the hour. The manager can check through your numbers, see how much stuff you pulled. (One-year backroom worker)

And also for cashiers:

> There is a score, how fast I take care of the guest. If I take a longer time I get an R [red], which means bad, or a G [green], which means good. If I get an R my score goes down a point so every day when I come I put my number in the main system and at the end they can see who did more service or better service or faster service for the guest. (First-year cashier)

In addition to these individual output measures, sales were measured for the store as a whole and ranked against a daily goal, which, as at Macy's, was calculated using that store's year-to-date sales plus an incremental increase. "Do they ever break it down by department?" I asked a first-year saleswoman. "No" she told me, "the pharmacy is separate and they add that in later, and then

Food Avenue [café], but the sales goals are for the whole store. . . . If we are consistently not making sales goals, then they are going to be short on giving people hours and pay. . . . So they usually talk about that, like we need to get our sales up and then we can get our hours up."

Taken together, the subdivision and prespecification of service and maintenance tasks, combined with multiple electronic measures of individual and store-level output, constituted a system of technical control that was more robust than Macy's, which only loosely preprogrammed customer service (MAGIC selling) and measured individual, departmental, and store-level sales. But Target's rules and methods went beyond technical organization. They bridged into "the social and organizational structure of the firm" and "establishe[d] the impersonal force of 'company rules' or 'company policy'" (Edwards 1979, 131). This was bureaucratic control, evidenced by three sets of rules: "compliance" and being "brand," performance reviews, and department- and store-level grading carried out by corporate representatives. Compliance encompassed employee dress code, attendance, meal and rest breaks, and interpersonal behavior. When workers were in compliance, they were said to be brand, which could also refer to the condition of the store—whether displays conformed to corporate guidelines. "The rules," said a three-year in-stock worker who had also worked in the backroom and as a salesman, "are that you have to go on your break at a certain time to stay in compliance, meaning that you don't get a write-up from the managers. . . . Once you are out of compliance you have to sign a document stating you were out of compliance, and if you get three out-of-compliances you get a write-up, and . . . if you have three write-ups you can get fired." "Hitting compliance," as a first-year salesman put it, most often meant violating shift-time and rest-break rules, which were fine-tuned to match federal and state laws. It could also refer to dress code: "a red top (any shade of red is fine, but not orange, pink or purple) and solid color pants or skirts (preferably khaki)" followed by eleven types of clothing under the heading "Don't wear" (Target Corporation 2008, 21). Attendance: "If you are absent three scheduled days in a row without calling your team leader . . . you will be considered to have voluntarily terminated your employment with Target" (ibid.). And finally, compliance also referred to the company's "Drug-Free-," "Violence-Free-" and "Harassment-Free Workplace" policies (ibid., 46–51). Violation of any of these could result in a write-up or immediate dismissal, depending on the severity of the infraction or the supervisor's disposition.

Write-ups also affected workers' annual reviews. Reviews took place ninety days after each employee's start date and then once a year for everyone. The process consisted of team leaders sitting down with team members and discussing their "performance and attendance—those are the two most important things" (three-year in-stock worker), which determined raises, promotions, and grounds for dismissal. Dismissal, however, could happen any time if the worker had three write-ups, consecutive absences, or a serious compliance violation, such as fighting in the store. Promotions also happened throughout the year "as positions bec[a]me available" (Target Corporation 2008, 29).

The final aspect of bureaucratic control at Target consisted in the department and store-level grading carried out by corporate management. Customer surveys were one mechanism: completed online, these were tallied up to produce a red, yellow, or green service rating for each store—green being the best, yellow in the middle, and red the worst. Service ratings reflected on workers as a group (though not as individuals) and were discussed with them by managers.

The general effect of these mechanisms was a lower level of autonomy for Target's workers than for Macy's. Combined with greater division of labor, standardization, collectivization, and more frequent rotation among roles, the organization of work at Target mirrored Toyotist principles of manufacturing in a service environment.

THIS CHAPTER INTERROGATED work design at two modern department stores and found two distinct sales regimes: eroded craft at Macy's and service Toyotism at Target. Macy's had a decentralized sales process and specialized salespersons whose customer interaction was highly individualized. They deployed product knowledge and persuasion to guide customers toward purchase, evincing forms of deep acting (Hochschild 1983), but semi-self-service and branding had eroded their skills in comparison with those required in prewar department stores (Benson 1986). In contrast, Target's process was much more centralized, while interactive tasks were collectivized and mechanized—aided by devices that cued workers' tasks and connected them with inventory databases. Target salespersons deployed little to no product knowledge and never closed purchases, performing surface acting similar to that of fast-food servers (Leidner 1993).

How do these models compare to the long-studied history of manufacturing? Macy's paralleled the handicraft factories of early industrialism, where workers were housed under one roof but worked mostly independently. Target stores, for their part, more closely resembled the flexibilized mass production of the post-Fordist (or Toyotist) auto plant: workers contributed in various partial ways to a streamlined, just-in-time process that was thoroughly predefined by management. But both craft and Toyotist models depended upon more than functional organization—they were buttressed by enabling social relations.

4

Carrots, Sticks, and Workers

THE RELATIONS OF EMPLOYMENT

The last chapter showed how workers in two service environ-ments expended their energy every day. Macy's salespersons worked in an individualized and relatively skilled fashion, while Target workers performed their more simplified tasks collectively and with greater aid from technology. With a few minor exceptions, these processes repeated themselves uninterrupted and, at the time of writing, generated enough profit for each firm to remain in busi-ness. Why did workers do this? Why did they, as Burawoy (1979) once asked, "work as hard as they do"? From an employer's per-spective, this is the problem of turning human labor power into value-producing labor. Its solution typically involves incentives. To the extent employers provide high wages, benefits, or recognition, they can be said to seek consent—to use carrots rather than sticks. But to the extent they threaten job loss or reduced hours or wages, they can be said to wield a coercive stick. In practice, most use a mix of both. And workers, in turn, have diverse expectations: a mean-ingful incentive to one might be unimportant to another.

Here I examine how Macy's and Target motivated workers on the sales floor. Parallel to the regulation approach (discussed in chapter 2) which distinguished between economic "regimes of ac-cumulation" and normative "modes of regulation," this chapter considers the latter within the microcosm of the service work-place. I compare four aspects of each firms' normative regime—material incentives (wages, hours, and job security), working conditions, managerial style, and unionism—followed by the life positions of workers and how these intersect with such policies. Both Macy's and Target, it can be said, were low-wage employers. But Macy's wage floor was fully two dollars lower than that of non-union Target. Job security was higher at unionized Macy's than at either company's nonunion stores, while working conditions were typically worse and supervisory styles more authoritarian at Macy's, regardless of unionization. Target, however, deployed sophisticated union-prevention tactics that included video screen-ings, one-on-one meetings, and, according to some, undercover surveillance. Macy's also took steps to prevent organizing at its nonunion stores, but where unions were established, accommoda-tion prevailed. A key difference was that Macy's employed a mix of older and younger workers, while Target's workforce was predomi-nantly young and transient. I argue these differences constituted a broadly adversarial culture at Macy's and a broadly paternalistic one at Target, yet the coercive sticks of termination and hour re-duction were still well-known at Target, as were the security car-rots achieved through collective bargaining at Macy's.

Wages, Hours, and Job Security

One prominent living wage estimate for a single adult in New York City was $12.75 at the time of study—assuming full-time, year-round employment. For a family of four (two adults and two children), the figure was $22.32 (Glasmeier 2012). Of the forty-four Macy's workers I interviewed, only one, a thirty-one-year noncommissioned salesman, earned more than the family-of-four estimate. More than two-thirds (thirty) earned less than the single-adult estimate, and seven of these worked part-time rather than full-time. The lowest wage reported at Macy's was $7.40 (at a nonunion store), and some workers at unionized stores noted pay of just $7.50, confirmed by Local 1-S president Ken Bordieri (New York's minimum was then $7.25). At Target the lowest reported wage was $9.50, while the highest was $11.10 for a two-year electronics salesman. Several Target workers also noted a cap of $11.50 for team members. What explains these differences, and how did they intersect with those in benefits, hours, and job security?

At Macy's higher pay accrued to those with higher seniority or those paid on commission, who received $8 an hour plus $150 to $500 weekly, depending on sales. Most Macy's subjects, however, earned less than $12, making their employment a low-wage endeavor. A two-year commissioned saleswoman, among the higher-paid at Macy's, described her struggle to support herself and her daughter in high-rent New York:

> *A:* For rent you have to save up for maybe three weeks just to make it and if one week you do less [commissioned sales] then you debate whether you should put some of that towards rent. It's that level of living.
>
> *Q:* What proportion of your income would you say goes towards rent?
>
> *A:* I think that's all I'm really paying. I live at my father's house. If I was in the world I wouldn't be able to pay it.

A four-year noncommissioned saleswoman, who worked full-time and lived by herself, relied on public assistance:

> I make $9.15 an hour. I can't get Medicaid because I make too much for Medicaid, so I'm damned if I do and I'm damned if I don't. The best I can do is drop some of my hours and go part-time. And if I

go part-time I still got other bills in life that I have to pay, so now I'm gonna have to depend on the city to help me. Believe it or not, I already have the city helping me pay my rent and everything. They pay me half and I appreciate that. I have to pay the other half because I'm working.

A two-year commissioned salesman stated that "if you have a family to provide for you are going to take [commissions] pretty serious." To him, however, "it's just another job to have while I'm in college. I'm still living at home so it's just something to keep money in my pocket."

Macy's provided little in the way of benefits. Approximately half of Local 1-S's four thousand members were eligible for the company's health plan, but only half of those—about one thousand—were actually enrolled. The reason? "It really sucks and is really expensive," explained Bordieri. Since the concessionary 1994 contract following Macy's bankruptcy, workers have contributed toward the health plan if enrolled; since 1999, as Bordieri pointed out, they "have been asked to pay 50 percent or even 54 percent." The result was that many either had no health insurance or sought it elsewhere. One eleven-year saleswoman said, "They do have a health plan for part-timers but it's far too expensive for me." As the four-year saleswoman quoted above explained, "You can have health insurance with Macy's, but it's too expensive. For me, because I am single, it's $59.68 the last time I read on the paper and that's a week, not a month. . . . That's a little steep for a person who's making $9.15 an hour—that's a big part of my salary." Benefits at nonunion stores were largely the same. A first-year merchandiser noted that the basic health plan cost "about $250 a month," and while unionized workers prior to 1994 had been offered defined-benefit pensions, they were now offered the same 401(k) plan as their nonunion counterparts, which most declined.

Hours and job security were different. Unionized Macy's workers had more stable schedules and stronger protection from dismissal than their nonunion peers. Full-time union workers were guaranteed 37.5 hours per week, part-time workers 20, and short-hour workers 12. In 2011, Macy's management tried reducing full-time hours from 37.5 to 28, which, according to Bordieri, "got people out on the street" for two rallies at the four unionized stores. Macy's then abandoned this effort, but a long-term strategy could be seen in its erosion of full-time employees. According to several respondents, Macy's had hired more and more short-hour workers, and Bordieri believed the company's "long-term goal is no guaranteed full-time hours." His belief was borne out at nonunion stores. There, all "nonpermanent" employees—a status lasting up to a year—were on "flex-time": "They give me four hours," explained a first-year saleswoman. "Yeah, four hours [per week]. I have to fill in all those gaps to get 30 hours." Full-time "permanent" workers typically received "35 to 40 hours per week" (two-year saleswoman), but all others got only token official hours, then had to schedule themselves wherever possible using the smart phone app MySchedule.

Unionized workers also had considerable job security. A "five-year wage and salary guarantee" stipulated that in the event of layoffs, any member with at least five years' employment was guaranteed a job at the same rate of pay. And supervisors had to follow lengthy protocols to fire anyone. An assistant manager found the process "extremely hard," and a one-year salesman concurred: "As long as you're not crazy, not always calling out or stealing, it could take a year and a half to actually get fired." Not so at nonunion stores. "They fired forty-five people right after the [CEO of Macy's Terry] Lundgren visit," stated a first-year merchandiser. "We were like 'why did the overtime hours decrease so suddenly?' Because the visit is over and we got rid of all these extra people."

Working at Target was also low-wage but for entry-level workers not as low. Starting pay was $9.50 at the stores I studied—a full two dollars higher than at unionized Macy's. But Macy's wages ranged into the twenties and were higher on average than Target's. A first-year saleswoman who was also a part-time teacher had this to say about supporting herself solely from her Target income: "There is no way. I have a mortgage, I have a brand new car, there is just no way I would make it at all. If I can't make it on my teaching paycheck there is no way I would be able to make it on a Target paycheck." A one-year salesman who made $9.50 remarked that "this is hand to mouth, you know what I mean? This is just keeping what I need to survive, this can't buy me a house." "I guess it is good for a teenager," said a first-year saleswoman who earned $9.60. When I pointed out that she was in fact twenty-four and had a bachelor's degree, she admitted, "No, it's not really doing anything for me. I feel that I should be in the double digits by now. I don't have kids or anything so what I am making now is good for me. If I had a child, then this $9.60 would not be cutting it."

When I asked about benefits, things at first seemed different. "We have a health insurance, we have dental and all that," said an eleven-year saleswoman. "Yes they do," replied a first-year saleswoman to the same question; "they give health, dental, 401(k) plan, holidays, sick days, vacation days, just ask in advance and they will give it to you." "You can [get health insurance]," said the saleswoman and part-time teacher, "if you are consistently working the whole year twenty hours or more a week." But appearances were deceiving. The eleven-year saleswoman was not on Target's health plan: "I have Medicaid," she told me. The first-year saleswoman "didn't actually do [apply for] it yet," and the part-time teacher "g[o]t health insurance through my school, so I don't need it [from Target]." In fact, of the thirty-one Target workers interviewed, only one was enrolled in the company's health plan, and none were on the 401(k). "It's too expensive," said a seven-year saleswoman and single mother. "Since my pay is not big, I get Medicaid and food stamps, and I get child support for my son." Paid vacation and sick days were allotted by the number of hours worked per year. According to the same saleswoman, "the only way you could earn two weeks [vacation] is by never missing one day or calling out."

And it was difficult to accumulate hours or avoid calling out because weekly schedules constantly changed. Only the two Target specialists I interviewed had consistent forty-hour workweeks; the other twenty-nine had fluctuating schedules. "Team leads have full-time," said the saleswoman and teacher, "but anybody below the team leads, like me, no they don't." A one-year backroom worker described his situation in February: "It's the slow time of the year so it would be like twenty-five, twenty, thirty [hours], it would go up and down like that." A one-year in-stock worker from the same store said, "I get thirty-eight, thirty-five, thirty-eight, thirty-five [hours], I don't go below that," except during "the low season, then you hit thirty, twenty-nine, thirty-one. It is not regular, it is not stabilized, it keeps changing." Unstable hours created unstable pay. This is what Lambert (2008) calls "passing the buck"—the costs—of market volatility onto employees, creating flexible schedules that meet customer demand but not workers' needs. A one-year saleswoman found this almost common sense: "It's retail. They schedule you according to how the system operates, according to their needs."

Job security was almost as tenuous as scheduling at Target. Turnover was high: "I've seen a lot of people come and go," said a four-year salesman. "I would say probably 85 percent of the team members that are here now weren't here when I started." A three-year specialist and former team leader saw this as systemic:

> The higher in management you go the less it changes. The lower it goes the more it changes, all the way down to team members because team members can go like this [snaps his fingers]. Supervisors come and go a little less frequently, managers [ETLs] go even less frequently and then you have the senior executives and the store team lead who have been the same since the store opened.

Formal dismissal was possible given three write-ups or a violation of compliance, but the same specialist also described a less formal process:

> They will try to manage you out. . . . This guy, he could work any day of the week except Saturday because he goes to church [then]. The manager is the type who likes to shake things up so he will give him no other days except Saturday, so he has to call out every week. And what happens if he does that? He will get fired. So they put you in a checkmate situation.

Because there was no union, workers could not appeal dismissals, hour reductions, or such arbitrary treatment. A three-year instock worker believed "a lot of people get fired about nonsense because we don't have a union."

In sum, both Macy's and Target were broadly low-wage employers that provided workers few attainable benefits and little scheduling or job security. Only unionized Macy's workers had guaranteed work time and protection from dismissal, which management had already tried (unsuccessfully) to curtail in 2011. Both firms thus offered more sticks than carrots, a pattern that bore little resemblance to the "family wage" welfarism of Sears or New York's highly organized stores in the postwar era.

Working Conditions

Any workplace, be it craft-based, Fordist, or Toyotist, can be well supplied, well staffed, and well run—or not. "Working conditions" refers to these factors and the deprivations workers suffer if they are lacking. Alongside wages, benefits, and security, working conditions have important effects on workers' consciousness, and many a strike has been fought over them. At Macy's I found that workers dealt with more unnecessary obstacles than did their Target peers. Both, however, cited sources of deprivation endemic to service jobs, such as constant standing, as well as more general problems like short-staffing, equipment malfunctions, and dirty facilities.

"I like working with people," stated a two-year Macy's saleswoman in her sixties.

> I just don't want to be doing this till I'm sixty-six. This is a very physical job. Even the young people have calluses—I thought I was the only one. I have these shoes, they worked for a little while and then my feet just started hurting again. I wouldn't recommend [this job] for seniors unless it's part-time, because it's too much pain.

A two-year specialist in her late twenties found that "the biggest challenges is the strenuous hours and the consistency of standing up all day"; and a two-year saleswoman in her fifties simply stated, "Yeah, it's tough to be on your feet." Retail selling, like much frontline service work, demands considerable physical exertion from workers. Though others have taken note of this (e.g., Lopez 2010), Macy's work displayed its continuing centrality within the emotional labor process.

But some discomforts were specific to Macy's. "I really don't like their facilities," said the one-year assistant manager. "The locker room has rats in it. It's probably the biggest retail store in the world and they have rats in the locker rooms. The cafeteria is not too good, it's horrible, it smells in there. The bathrooms too, it's not clean in there, the locker rooms suck."

A two-year saleswoman at a different store also noted "a rat problem, real bad. Where I work there was a bad odor—they found three dead rodents." Such disorganization could get in the way of sales. "To me one of the flaws in the system," stated a two-year saleswoman who previously worked at Target, "is that there is just merchandise everywhere; it's overwhelming how much stuff is in the hallways that the customers can't get at." "If the shop is really messy," said a first-year specialist, "who wants to shop there?"

Keeping stores clean was often difficult. According to a four-year saleswoman, "today there was supposed to be four of us, but sometimes you are short-staffed and there's only two of you until 2:30 and then the crowd comes in." Short-staffing reduced overall labor costs but may have also reduced sales. "Our store is struggling," remarked a ten-year specialist. "Customers are sick and tired of the long lines. We have no control over that—operations controls how many staff they have on a certain floor. Customers are always complaining that we don't have enough staffing because the workload is too much for us." A first-year specialist observed that "when you are short-staffed . . . you can't really help the customers." And a two-year saleswoman found that while support workers used to set up displays in the mornings, "now it's extending all day, people are shuffling around with racks, leaving them in your area." Short-staffing's frequent mention by workers across departments and stores—union and nonunion—suggested its prevalence throughout Macy's.

Short-staffing was also a common complaint at Target. "If I open," said a one-year specialist, "someone else will close. They won't know what they are doing and I will come in in the morning and have to fix everything." A two-year cashier felt there was "sometimes no communication between floors," which made it hard to check prices for customers: "There are times when we are left with no walkie, no PDA, so we have to call the department and wait and wait—I had a guest wait almost half an hour for a price." If items were falsely priced, explaining this fell to cashiers. "That's a problem that guests sometimes don't understand—maybe people in Target put the wrong item on the wrong shelf," a first-year cashier pointed out; "they get upset with me because it's $6.99," said a two-year cashier, "which is not really my fault, because I have nothing to do with the pricing." Problems at one point thus had ripple effects further down, often culminating at the registers. And this was occasionally aggravated by malfunctions. "A lot of the register lines are messed up," said the same two-year cashier, "so that means customers can't use them. We only have twenty-six lanes so seven of them are messed up. . . . You have twenty-five cashiers and only certain ones can get in the lane. The other ones are considered 'breakers'—they give other people breaks." The volume of customers at New York City Target stores was also very high, which strained the inventory system and tested workers' ability to keep up. "Everybody here is just so fast," said a first-year saleswoman who had previously worked at a suburban Target in Oregon. "Boom, boom, boom, mine, mine, mine, help me, help me. In [Oregon] there is not as much going on in the store as there is here. People buy so much here, so maybe some have had a bad experience when nothing is in stock. I get that a lot—'nothing is in stock here!' Forget Saturday, it's probably all gone!"

Target management attempted to match staffing levels as closely as possible to this ebb and flow of customers, but this was a calculated guessing game that often yielded underserved sales floors.

The complex compliance rules that largely consisted in telling workers when to take legally mandated breaks were stretched to their limits in these situations. "With the breaks they have this time grid to tell us when to go," said a two-year cashier,

> and they don't follow it. They come over to you and ask, "can we push it back like five or ten minutes?" Fine, but a lot of the times when it is that time you see on the paper and you go for your break, they ask you, "where are you going?" Well, I'm going for my break. "You can't [they say], you have to wait until someone comes and relieves you."

"Not that they are understaffed," said a three-year cashier, "but if they gave us better hours everything could overlap so there would always be coverage." A first-year saleswoman described working "double shifts, about twelve or thirteen hours" to cover such gaps. She also recounted a recent early-morning call-in: "My team lead calls me at 7:30 in the morning and was like, 'can you come into work right now?' and I was like 'come on' so she was like, 'okay, come in at ten.'" Call-in shifts were common at Target, reflecting the just-in-time and often harried nature of its sales process. "They will just call you and ask if you can come in," said a first-year saleswoman.

Last but equally important, physical deprivation was much the same at Target as at Macy's. "It's a lot of walking, it's a lot of being on your feet," said a three-year in-stock worker. An eleven-year saleswoman, herself over sixty, found it "stressful because you stand in one place; I don't like that." And a four-year cashier in her mid-thirties remarked that "by the time I get home my feet are hurting so bad." Stresses and strains of this sort were common, but reports of serious injury or severe discomfort were not. Unsanitary conditions, unlike at Macy's, were never mentioned.

On the whole, the experience of work at Target was somewhat less adverse than that at Macy's, where workers more often complained of supply, maintenance, and sanitation problems. Yet both groups struggled equally with short-staffing and the bodily fatigue of moving around the sales floor for hours on end. At Target, short-staffing also put greater drag on workers' ability to complete tasks because of their collectivized and interdependent nature.

Managerial Style

The manager's role is to coach and work with you, but I don't feel that they coach and work with us. They micromanage you. It's a tough environment—it's retail tough, retail tough. (Seven-year salesman, unionized Macy's)

Everything is pretty open, the team leads who are over me are pretty open. I don't feel that they are just like me—they are a step ahead of me but they don't try to use their authority over me. (Two-year cashier, Target)

How supervisors treat workers often contributes toward alienation or contentment. Here I compare Macy's managers' adversarialism with Target managers' teamwork approach. The former, however, could not be attributed entirely to unionization, since workers at nonunion Macy's had nearly identical experiences. Deviations from each pattern were also evident, with some Macy's workers citing support and some of their Target peers complaining of abuse. But overarching differences between the two firms' managerial styles were marked and palpable.

Macy's supervisors treated older, "career" employees—who had greater protection and typically worked in higher-skill departments—with greater hostility than younger, "short-term" workers.

"I've had my manager say something about my religion," said an eight-year saleswoman and shop steward, "and I filed a grievance on it and then he was like, 'I didn't say that!'" A two-year commissioned saleswoman found that "it is mostly negative feedback, stuff like you are not wearing your name tag or not wearing fully black . . . and it's so often." When I asked the thirty-one-year salesman whether managers had a standard approach toward sales staff, he said, "It depends on the manager—they will just sit down and do their own thing but eventually it's 'tell him or her to do this' and that's it." A three-year commissioned salesman noted, "There are very few people who go from a sales associate to being a manager. I think they want to keep that distance." And the seven-year salesman quoted above found the relationship "absolutely horrible. At this store there's people working twenty-five, forty years and they don't get the respect of seniority, managers don't honor that, they are terrible." Distance, formality, and hostility were common experiences among older, higher-skilled Macy's workers.

But younger, less skilled workers often experienced a different side. "My manager is wonderful; I like him," said a twenty-year-old, one-year specialist. "He's really nice and understanding and is easy to work with," she continued. "He's the type that will help you go up and go someplace else—he will promote you." "Managers have been really helpful," remarked an eighteen-year-old stock worker about his training. "Some of them can get under your skin, especially if they yell at you a lot, but I haven't been yelled at a lot." A first-year saleswoman in her early twenties found managers "pretty good, [they're] pretty casual and friendly. They want you to do your best but they can get a bit annoying because they sound like a broken record telling you to get star rewards, network customers, blah, blah, blah." Younger and older workers described department meetings and morning rallies where managers "try to keep us motivated, give us food or coffee, so that you could be yourself—your retail self," said a first-year salesman. Managers gave out praise, "recognition cards," and "Macy's money" (discount coupons) for high sales at these meetings, as well as for proper use of MAGIC. A two-year salesman noted "they tell you who met their goal, who was outstanding, stuff like that. And they give recognition, a recognition card—sort of a morale thing." The assistant manager encountered earlier, himself in his early twenties, described his own approach: "I speak with them, laugh with them, joke with them, but still make sure they are doing their job. They like interaction. . . . I try to joke with them and say, 'I used to be one of you guys, I know where you're coming from.'"

But even for younger workers management encounters were not always so laid-back. A two-year support worker at first said, "Managers treat workers good" but then described the following episodes:

> Recently one of my coworkers needed foot surgery and my manager was like, "oh it's nothing, it's not that painful, just make sure you come to work on Friday." When I used to work over here [different department] I had a fever one day and I threw up, the manager was still texting me, "are you going to come?" They don't see anything else, they just want people to come in and work.

This ambiguity suggests slow movement by Macy's toward the team-based style more pronounced at Target. Such an approach, however, was limited by both established unionism at some stores and the competitive, individualized sales process at all of them. Quotas and their attainment were a constant point of friction. The one-year specialist who found her manager "wonderful" still noted, "If my scorecard is really low, my manager will pull me aside and say, 'Hey, what's going on?'"

Target managers were more systematic. Their four-pronged approach involved informal banter, an "open-door" policy, team building and low-cost welfarism. These succeeded far more than at Macy's in creating a "vertical culture of unity" but were not without limits (Jacoby 1997, 53). A three-year Target food server had "seen a lot of other companies [where] managers talk to people like they are dirt. But they don't do that here; they don't talk to you like you dirt." "It's a very good relationship," said a one-year backroom worker about his supervisors. "We are very close, we are able to talk to them." A first-year salesman found the relationship "friendly, it's comfortable," and during another interview a woman walked by wearing Target's outfit: "She is one of my managers," explained the first-year saleswoman. "She's cool. She is always bothering me and I always bother her. It's a joke, we just joke around."

Many Target interviewees described their supervisors in similarly effusive terms: "cool," "friendly," "chill," "like family." The consistency of such reports was too great to dismiss as happenstance. Rather, supervisors' approach reflected a deliberate style encouraged by the company's corporate leaders. "Being Friendly," stated the employee handbook, "is lending a hand, talking through a problem, offering to listen and letting your own personality shine through"; one page later it praised a "culture where team members can feel comfortable talking honestly with leadership" (Target Corporation 2008, 9). Though such statements are not uncommon in many corporations' documents, Target appeared to do a better job than most at translating them into practice.

"Close" and "friendly" management, however, could sometimes feel like micromanaging. "I wanted to transfer out," explained a one-year specialist, "and they . . . just wanted me to stay forever, like a mother who won't let go of their child." A two-year cashier found managers' informal style condescending: "A lot of them speak to you like a child and I am an adult with my own kids. I don't even talk to my kids the way they talk to me." A four-year salesman found that to avoid reprimand, "you've got to be doing something, you've got to be communicating with your managers consistently," and a first-year saleswoman and former Macy's employee thought managers were equally tone-deaf at both companies: "It's like once they get hired as managers they get all this power and now they don't know how to talk to you like a person."

One mechanism for encouraging cooperation was Target's "open door policy." Simply stated, it meant "you can go to any leader with your thoughts or concerns" (Target Corporation 2008, 37). Employee input was sought through annual surveys, an "Employee Relations and Integrity Hotline," through anonymous suggestion boxes at each store, and at daily "huddles." A two-year salesman referred to it as "that open-door policy where any team member can just walk into the office." In practice, however, he found "they do prefer you go to the team lead you are assigned to as a first encounter." A four-year cashier knew about the policy but admitted, "I don't really know how it works. If I got a problem I just keep it to myself."

Huddles were another channel for input and a prime means of imbuing workers with a team ethos that transcended the workplace hierarchy. A storewide huddle took place each morning at eight, and "each section has their own little huddle throughout the day," said a first-year backroom worker. Storewide sales goals and their attainment (or not) were discussed at these, as well as any new display building, stocking, or customer service projects. But in addition, noted a first-year saleswoman, team leaders "talk about if it's somebody's birthday or if somebody has an anniversary, and they will give us samples from Starbuck's if there is a new drink." Team members were recognized by team leaders or coworkers for doing good work or reprimanded, by team leaders only, for hitting compliance. A first-year backroom worker described the latter: "If you hit compliance your name is also called—it's like public embarrassment. Nobody really looks at it that way but that's exactly what it is; they point you out in front of everybody and say, 'you messed up so you need to fix that.'" Some found the huddle helpful: "We actually get a breakdown," said a one-year salesman. "We get a perspective on what's going to happen that very day." The first-year saleswoman and former Macy's employee remarked that "Macy's just had one huddle in the morning but didn't have anything for the evening shift," as at Target. Cashiers, however, were excluded from most huddles, which although promoted as forums for worker input—approximating the "quality circles" of Japanese auto makers—were largely manager-run: "They are pretty open to suggestions," remarked the first-year saleswoman and teacher, "but nobody really says too much in the huddles besides the team leads—they are usually telling us what to do in the backroom or why hours are not being dispersed to everybody because we are not making sales goals."

A final aspect of Target's style was its low-cost welfarism. Although it offered workers few substantial benefits, such as health care, living wages, or pensions, "sometimes we have cereal day," said a first-year salesman, "where they have a bunch of cereal in the break room. They have a milk and cookies day, things like that. A lot of people don't have money to buy food every day, so there is always stuff in the break room, like peanut butter and jelly with bread." A three-year food server who received Medicaid noted, "You could have a chip day, or cookies, or something just to say thanks for your hard work. . . . Then tomorrow we might have burger day or hotdogs. That's a great thing because some people can't bring lunch to work!" Each store also provided a "counselor" whom employees were encouraged to visit. "If anything is going on at home," said a first-year salesman, "for whatever reason you can go in and talk." The goals of these efforts appeared twofold: encouraging cooperative relations between workers and managers while ameliorating the hardships of low-wage work. In the case of those who welcomed free food because they could not afford it themselves, Target's second goal seemed met.

Macy's managers were on the whole more adversarial than Target's, though they applied this style unevenly among older and younger workers. They did deploy some elements of team building, such as morning rallies and public praise, yet the robust package of welfarism, open-door-ism, and pseudotherapy found at Target was absent at union and nonunion Macy's. This divergence was thus more likely the result of corporate culture than of union presence. But when it came to workers' ability to bargain and assert their rights, divisions ran not between firms but between union and nonunion workplaces.

Unionism and Antiunionism

At the start of this chapter I showed how Local 1-S guaranteed job and hours security for its members though little in the way of wages. Union presence also shaped the dynamics of management interactions, giving workers leverage to question assignments and sales-floor directives. Nonunion Macy's and Target workers had no such ability, and their respective managements worked hard to keep them from getting it. At Target these union prevention efforts were more systematic, indicating a broader strategy than the ad hoc though no less effective one at nonunion Macy's.

What kind of union was Local 1-S? Was it an activist organization with rank-and-file participation? Or was it just another "business union" that delegated grievances to paid staffers and had little shop-floor presence? The accounts of several of its members, including three shop stewards, depict a union that was more than a shell. Local 1-S had numerous elected shop stewards who, along with staffers, were seen by many members as accessible and helpful when problems arose. Because of this, the union was able to uphold the integrity of its contracts between negotiating rounds, which came every five years. The problem was that the terms of those contracts had declined considerably since the mid-1990s.

"Sometimes the manager tells you to do things we are not supposed to do," said an eleven-year saleswoman. "In that case you go to the shop steward, who gives you a suggestion. Then we meet about it, talk about it, make a copy of [the suggestion] and have the manager sign it." "We kind of broke down the managers to where they have to respect us," stated an eight-year saleswoman and shop steward. "Instead of being more confrontational with workers they try to be more understanding." On her floor, there were four shop stewards covering five departments. "It should be like five," she said, "but it's only four." Some had only two, "and some floors didn't have any" because, according to the same woman, "you have fifty-fifty: 50 percent of people that care [about the union] and 50 percent that don't." A different shop steward and seven-year salesman described how he came to fill that position:

> After I worked here for a couple of years I started to have issues with management and I submitted my first grievance. I went over to the union [office], sat down with one of the union administrators and talked about the issues and they said, "why don't you become a shop steward?" And I was like, that's too

much work . . . but I left and thought maybe I really should. So I got voted in and with all the issues going on in my store I became prounion and progrievance—that issues need to be put on paper.

"Without shop stewards we don't have an organization," stated Ken Bordieri. These individuals were the first line of defense against arbitrary treatment and contract violations. A two-year saleswoman noted that "if a manager is going to talk to you, you have the option of taking a shop steward with you for protection." A first-year specialist saw her steward "pretty much every day. . . . If we ever have a problem with the managers he will be there to help us or to tell them 'this is not right.'"

In June 2011, Local 1-S held "two major rallies before the actual vote on whether we would strike. They also have a Facebook page for our local—that's how I knew . . . whether we were going to strike or not" (two-year salesman). A first-year support worker described contact with union officials at that time: "A lady [from the union] came in and told me they were having a meeting and somebody told me about the strike. I was excited because I was supposed to work that day. . . . Then I called my manager and he said, 'get your ass here because the store is not closed.'" And a first-year commissioned saleswoman found that union membership, obtained after a ninety-day probation period, made a positive difference:

> Before I was in the union they [managers] used to give me crazy schedules and if I asked to change they would be like, "just work the hours." But after I became part of the union [they] would call the managers right away and be like, "why are you giving her this schedule?" As soon as they get that call they get scared and change the schedule. If you have any issue you can always go to the union; they are always there to help.

These experiences and many like them display Local 1-S as present and helpful. But not all workers felt the same. A two-year support worker believed "the main people [the 2011 contract] affected were people who have been here fifteen or twenty years," rather than newer employees like him. A first-year specialist said she had little interaction with or need for the union "because I came in, worked hard and the manager recognized me—it works for me." And a four-year specialist commented, "union people? They pop up when the election comes and after the election it's hard to find them. You have to go to the head office, sometimes on the phone they are too busy and honestly, the union thing? I don't like it. But yeah, sometimes it saves your job." Those who expressed such ambivalence were often either unfamiliar with unions or convinced of their ability to bargain independently. Others, however, were generally prounion but faulted Local 1-S for specific shortcomings. The thirty-one-year salesman held that "we could've had a better union. They go too much with the company. We just got a contract in June and a sixty-five-cent raise for five years. . . . They don't care for workers anymore." Regarding to the quota system, the seven-year salesman and shop steward stated, "I don't think the union has put up enough resistance." Frustration with retreats on pay, benefits, and output monitoring also coexisted with appreciation for the union's defense of job security and shop-floor respect: "The only thing that the union helps you with," said a ten-year specialist, "is your raise once a year and it sucks. The raise really sucks. But the union is a good thing, because it makes sure that we are secure with what they offer us—makes sure nobody abuses us, makes sure that the schedule is consistent."

At nonunion Macy's, there were no shop stewards. If you had a complaint, "you go visit HR and she [the HR manager] will talk it out, ask you if you want to complain," said a two-year saleswoman.

But job security was much less assured—especially if one was seen to be prounion. The same two-year saleswoman relayed what she had heard about a previous attempt to organize: "They [the union] tried and then the managers and the boss got everybody. . . . I heard that everybody who was trying to get with the union was getting let go. People got scared and the managers told them that they got fired because they was signing with the union." A first-year saleswoman described a firsthand experience: "The union always tries to talk to you and then the managers just give you this look like 'you best not say yes to any of this shit.'" I asked whether she had been approached by organizers: "Yeah, like once," she replied, "but every time we have a meeting [afterwards] where the managers are like 'does anybody want to do the union or sign up?'" A first-year salesman noted that "in the training they said 'do not sign up for a union'" and another first-year saleswoman confirmed this: "They told us in our training that [union] people are going to come." A two-year saleswoman also said that "when I started orientation they showed us a video against unions."

Management at nonunion Macy's was clearly committed to keeping unions out. One-on-one discussions, preemptive dissuasion, threats of termination, and antiunion film screenings are standard parts of many firms' union-prevention schemes—and Macy's was no different. Target deployed similar techniques, but these were much more integrated into the company's teamwork approach. Indeed, a primary goal of Target's employment relations appeared to be union avoidance. The company's employee handbook succinctly states its "union philosophy":

> We believe in solving issues and concerns by working together with your help and input. Target wants to continue to create the kind of workplace where team members don't want or need union representation to resolve issues. We don't believe a union or any

third-party representative would improve anything for you, our guests or the company. There are a lot of great things that go along with being a Target team member and you don't need to go to an outside party to get them. (Target Corporation 2008, 18–19)

"It's no secret," said a one-year salesman, "Target doesn't do unions." A first-year saleswoman who had once worked at a unionized Macy's in Maryland noted, "I didn't really hear too much about union organization until I started working here at Target." Several expressed fear of being fired or having their hours cut if managers found out they were prounion, such as the one-year backroom worker who had to clarify I was not an organizer before agreeing to talk. A first-year backroom worker at a different store stated that during the Valley Stream organizing drive in spring 2011, his managers

> had a discussion with us about union people coming to the store and asking whether we want to join or not. "If you choose to join the union by all means go ahead," [they said]. But after the discussion most of us were basically like "no" for the union. They even asked us, "would you want to join the union?" And they would speak to us individually; they would pick out certain people and talk to us about joining the union.

And the four-year saleswoman quoted in the first chapter described mandatory screenings of an antiunion video at the same time.

The video she saw was probably Target's thirteen-minute short film "Think Hard Before You Sign," widely accessible on the Internet. In it, a white man and black woman, both in team-member attire, walk viewers through a series of "facts" about unions, why they want to organize Target, and why this is "not in the best interest of the company or the team members." Target's open-door policy and teamwork philosophy are explicitly used to discourage workers from joining a union "or any third party": "our team environment," states Jim Rowader, Target's Director of Labor Relations, "strives to create a clear, direct path of communication." A graph depicting union decline since the 1950s is displayed while the actors recite reasons why unions were once important—"child labor," "health and safety"—but are now obsolete—"these are all laws today." The take-home is that unions are greedy businesses— "that's right, I said business," states the white male actor—that seek workers' dues without providing benefits. To underline this last claim, the black actress reminds viewers that "management can simply say 'no' to union demands," reaffirming their privileged role. The closing words are those of the male actor: "Refuse to sign . . . and keep Target union free."

Although use of this film and other prevention tactics peaked during the Valley Stream campaign, longer-term workers noted that similar initiatives had been used before. An eleven-year saleswoman recounted a time early in her tenure when "they tried to make Target a union [store] but they [management] didn't allow it—anybody that agreed with it would get fired."

Q: Did people come to the store and ask you to sign up for it?

A: Yeah, but you had to say no because they didn't want a union here.

Q: Did managers say you have to say no?

A: Yeah, because otherwise you get fired.

A three-year in-stock worker described a similarly abortive organizing drive at a different store:

A: They were trying to get a union but it didn't work out. . . . Some people was trying to get a union and they say that we don't need a union.

Q: Were you one of them?

A: No, I wasn't one of them.

Q: What happened to the people who were? Did they get fired?

A: No they didn't but most of them left. My one friend got fired because of misplaced keys, and some people because of attendance, too many call-outs, they got fired too. But some people call out every week and they are still on the job.

"Union people has come to the store," stated a seven-year saleswoman, herself a former union member, "and they said no, no, no, no. As one [supporter] from all the six hundred employees I would lose my job." She was "in favor of the union, but nobody else is." I asked why, and she explained,

They scared that they gonna lose their job, and they need the job. Like they [managers] will watch you if you speak to a union representative outside the store, and they do, they send people because they have undercovers working for the store. I know all of them but there's people that don't know them. I spoke with them [the undercovers] outside!

No one else mentioned undercover surveillance, though this is not unheard of at discount retailers (Adams 2006; Lichtenstein 2009, 118–48). But multiple accounts indicated that Target discouraged unionization through a range of tactics, and not just as short-term responses to "crisis situations." If workers were indeed fired for union activity, then both Macy's and Target clearly violated U.S. law as codified in the National Labor Relations Act. Egregious as such actions are, they are not uncommon among U.S. employers; their use supports Kochan, Katz, and McKersie's (1994) and Goldfield's (1987) arguments that union decline is a result of fierce employer resistance. The content of Target's anti-union overtures—their reference to teamwork and the open-door policy—also buttresses a prominent criticism of "participatory management": namely, that its goal is to prevent workers from organizing rather than simply fostering high performance (Hodson 1996; Milkman 1991).

The Workers Themselves

None of employers' carrots and sticks, however, can have their intended effects if workers are not somehow receptive (or vulnerable) to them. The financial positions, educational backgrounds, and family responsibilities of individuals thus play a key role in structuring their expectations as well as their tolerance for or resistance to authority. Here I explore the backgrounds of those I interviewed, drawing on the distinction between primary and secondary workers. Primary workers are those whose wages provide vital income, while secondary workers are not dependent on wages for most basic needs, such as housing and food. But although this dichotomy captured much of the difference in life positions among participants and helped explain their expectations, it was also limiting. Several fell between these two groups, while others appeared to be in one but had expectations more consistent with another. And Macy's and Target hired not only those they thought would accept their relational schemes but also those with the skills to sell effectively.

Macy's, union and nonunion, hired both primary and secondary workers, while Target almost exclusively sought the latter. A nonunion Macy's saleswoman in her forties found, "It's a struggle. I got this job, I have another part-time job, and I've got kids. . . . But I want to go back to school, back to college. It's mostly kids here who want to go to school, but full-timers, parents? I'm just here because there's nothing else I could do." And a unionized Macy's salesman in his twenties explained, "I haven't been here that long; this is my first official job. I'm actually applying for computer tech jobs, which is what I studied and what I wish to do for the rest of my life. But this is good—we get some benefits, some discounts." "I'm just working for metro card money because I go to school and I'm majoring in speech pathology," said a nonunion Macy's saleswoman in her early twenties. "I want to go into my field; I don't want to be doing this [long-term]."

Paths to working at Macy's were as numerous as the workers themselves. But among those interviewed three groups could be discerned, represented by the individuals above. First were those, typically middle-aged, who did not have a college degree and worked at Macy's because they had few better options. Second were those, often in their twenties but sometimes older, who had college credentials yet were unable to find jobs that matched and worked at Macy's as a stopgap. Third were younger workers currently in college who had considerable family support. The first, primary, group was once preponderant but now made up less than half of the workforce in Macy's stores (union and nonunion). These individuals were often in higher-value or commissioned sales departments, though not exclusively. The second and third groups had grown considerably by most accounts and were more evenly distributed among departments.

Samantha[1] was in the first group. At the time we spoke, she had worked at Macy's full-time for five years, first as a sales associate, then as a specialist. In the early 1990s she had emigrated from a small Caribbean nation to join her husband in New York. "My husband was here and he asked me to come up so I came," she

---

1. Not her real name. All further names are also pseudonyms.

related. "At first I babysat for quite a while because I didn't have my papers. Then this came along because in 2004 I got my green card." Samantha had an associate's degree, and her husband was the superintendent of an apartment building. "I read a lot," she told me. "I go to church. That's about it. I go from home to work to church." For Samantha, not working was not an option: earnings from Macy's were a key part of her household income.

Kelly's situation was similar, if more constrained financially. Born and raised in New York, she had worked at Macy's as a full-time specialist for almost a year when we talked, was in her late twenties and had a three-year-old daughter. "Macy's doesn't really care for your needs," she felt, "because if I need a day off to take my daughter somewhere, I have to call out and miss a day's pay." Like Samantha, Kelly did not have a bachelor's degree, but unlike her she also did not have a partner with whom to pool resources. Living with extended family provided her affordable housing and some child-care, but the situation was not ideal: "Sometimes when I get home my daughter is asleep and when I leave to go to work [in the morning] she's still asleep, and she goes, 'Mommy, I never see you!'"

These and others like them were primary retail workers: lack of college credentials excluded them from higher-paying office or managerial work, and they depended on Macy's wages for a large part of their income. They most often became "career" Macy's employees.

Others, however, were in between: they had college degrees but were unable to find college-level work. David was in this group. He graduated from a well-known university with a bachelor's in engineering and then pursued a master's but dropped out and returned to New York one summer. "I started looking for jobs in electrical engineering," he explained, "but I couldn't find anything.

Then sometime in December I got hired at Macy's as a seasonal for the holidays. They let me go in February. I did some other part-time jobs and then in September they called me back and hired me as a permanent [employee]." David had worked at Macy's as a part-time salesman in a commissioned department for three years. According to him, most of his colleagues "are either full-time and it doesn't look like they're going anywhere else, or part-time workers that have a full-time job somewhere else."

Allison was also in this group. A subcontracted visual merchandiser at Macy's and other area stores, she did not plan it that way. "The economy is bad," she said. "I am a fashion designer but there is no fashion work. So I had to switch to merchandising." She moved to New York from Florida to study fashion, working part-time as a Macy's salesperson. "When there are no jobs in design, you kind of have the skill set to get a job in merchandising—that's like the back-up." Allison supported herself, with some family help, from the hourly wages in her "part-time to full-time to overtime" position.

Several Macy's respondents were college students who lived with their parents. One of these, Sylvia, was born and raised in New York, had been a full-time specialist at Macy's for a little over a year, and was twenty years old. When not at work, she studied nursing. "You have a life, you have expenses and bills," she said, "and I can't live off nine dollars an hour. I still live with my mom, so thank God for that."

Hassan was also in college, studying business. His family had emigrated from Bangladesh, but he was born in New York. He had been a part-time support worker at Macy's for almost two years, before which he "worked at a Subway sandwich store, I worked at a Häagen-Dazs, and at a pharmacy for seven or eight months." Hassan "miss[ed] those days where I could wake up, lay in bed and take my time doing homework. Since two years ago every time I wake up it's either for school or work." But Macy's suited his present needs: there was "convenient scheduling, my manager understands me, everybody's friendly. The pay is not much but it's an easy job." Hassan earned ten dollars an hour.

In general, there was rough congruence between Macy's workers backgrounds and their expectations. Younger, secondary workers often wanted flexible, part-time hours and a fun, enjoyable workplace; they were not ambivalent about pay and benefits but could make due with less since their basic needs were met. Those in the intermediate group also wanted a conflict-free workplace but expected better pay and more hours than their secondary counterparts; they were more often unhappy with Macy's conditions, and more confident in asserting this through union channels. Long-term primary workers were the most confident in this regard and, unsurprisingly, had the highest expectations for pay and benefits. But whereas those in the first two groups rarely claimed their work was meaningful or sought recognition for it, primary workers did this often. They took pride in their knowledge and sales ability, seeing in retail more than a stepping-stone and struggling against its social devaluation.

Target workers differed from their Macy's peers in two ways: they were more often young and, at two of the stores I studied, more often Caribbean. The composition of Target's store-level workforces pointed toward a distinctly younger and more secondary group than at Macy's.

"This store is mostly Caribbean," said a four-year Target salesman. "A lot of people are Caribbean." When I asked a first-year saleswoman at the same store whether people of Caribbean origin made up a large portion of the workforce, she replied, "Yes, very large, very large; I think it's the location" (the store was adjacent to a mostly Caribbean neighborhood). The third Target store had a broader ethnic mix, but at all three a majority of workers were younger individuals who often enough were also students.

Kendra was one of these. She was twenty years old when we spoke and had recently earned an associate's degree in photography. "I live with my mom and my dad and my brother and my cousin and my uncle," she told me. Having worked at Target for a little under a year, Kendra did not pay her own rent but covered some utilities: "On Friday I had to pay my phone bill and my brother's phone bill and then I went out. But me, I spend my check the same day I get it," she continued. "I go shopping a lot—it's a problem." I asked if it would be hard to support herself on a Target income: "Yeah, I would have to have another job. I think this is enough for just rent, but no food and no clothes; I would have to stop shopping."

Davian—unlike Kendra, who was African American—was from the Caribbean. "I'm from Guyana," he said, "I came up here in 2005. I graduated high school there and then I came up here because there's really nothing to do there jobwise. My father sent [for] me because he was up here a long time before me, so I just came up here to go to school and try to find a better job." Davian was a junior in college and used his Target wages to pay tuition while living with his father. "The younger people like us," he said, "we just work and try to pay for school." He worked as close to full-time as he could, which was difficult "because sometimes they cut hours." "But I don't really stress," he said, "because I just want to make enough so I can pay for my school. The older people, they support their family off this," which he thought "has to be hard."

Kendra, Davian, and most other Target respondents were secondary workers: income from Target was not trivial—in Davian's case allowing him to pay for college—but it was also not needed for basic costs like housing and food. Yet many others did have to pay for these.

Amy was one such person. A public school teacher from Oregon, she was white, single, and forty years old. In 2010 had been diagnosed with cancer and later that year she lost her teaching job as a result of state budget cuts. She described her situation:

> I wasn't as stressed going through chemo and radiation as I was when I lost my job. I was like, what am I going to do? I needed insurance because I wasn't on any insurance; I would have to pay $720 a month to keep COBRA. I can't afford that, especially when I have a $1,000 mortgage. I applied to minimum wage jobs, Dick's Sporting-Goods, Macy's, and then when I saw the wages I was like, I can't take that as a full-time job.

To make ends meet she began working at a Target store in Oregon while substitute teaching. The following summer she transferred to a position at a store in New York. "I wanted to move out here and get a teaching job," she told me. "On my off days I try to find teaching jobs." Amy did not plan to stay at Target for longer than she had to.

Jonathan also saw Target as a short-term endeavor, and for him it could not be short enough. During his first two years he had advanced from team member to team leader while taking classes toward his bachelor's, which he had since attained. But when his son was born, it complicated this arrangement: "Some days I couldn't stay [late]; I had to watch my son. They gave me an ultimatum: keep going the way you are going and whatever happens happens, or you could leave now and come back." Jonathan took the second option and returned to Target several months later as a specialist. Before working at Target, Jonathan had held a union job as a traffic checker; he left it on the advice of his father, who said that with a college degree, he could do better. "To this day," said Jonathan, "I regret leaving that job."

Amy, Jonathan, and others like them were not short-term primary workers because their tenure at Target would inevitably be brief. They considered their current jobs short-term because their degrees qualified them for higher-paying work and they were actively seeking such an upgrade. Long-term primary workers lacked these credentials and at Target, as at Macy's, were mostly over thirty.

Sabina was in this group. Born in Puerto Rico, she was in her early fifties, had worked at Target for seven years, and had two children (one of whom was still a dependent). "At the age I am," she told me, "a lot of people don't want to hire [you]—it's the truth, they are hiring younger people." Before coming to Target, Sabina had worked at a unionized garment factory, "and before that I was sixteen years a bartender. It has its ups and downs," she said about Target, "but you keep your nose clean, you do what you have to do and you are fine." Sabina was able to secure thirty-two hours per week, sometimes more, through extensive cross-training and proactively seeking shifts when others called out. But she still qualified for Medicaid and lived in public housing. "It's not easy," she said. "I had to be a survivor, I had to be a bitch on wheels. If you have been a bartender for sixteen years and then after hours have to help your kids through school, you gotta be a fucked-up bitch." Sabina was not looking for other jobs when we spoke.

Macy's and Target elicited labor power in different ways. Though both provided few real carrots, Target provided more soft incentives like praise, recognition, food, and counseling. Union and nonunion Macy's employed aspects of this low-cost welfarism, including rallies and praise, but these did not cohere as systematically as at Target. The same could be said for nonunion Macy's union-prevention tactics: video screenings, preemptive dissuasion, and illegal intimidation all appeared in management's repertoire, but they were not linked to an embedded teamwork ethos. At unionized Macy's, management was forced to accommodate, granting workers job security and scheduling stability that their unorganized peers were denied. Both firms, however, were pushing as far as possible into the available pool of secondary workers while relegating many primary workers to secondary-type jobs. But Target was further ahead. In the next chapter, I argue that de-skilling made this possible and that both dynamics were part and parcel of a regime of contingent control.

5

A Regime of Contingent Control

The concerns that animate this book are the absence of unions in many frontline services, the dynamics of these workplaces, how they change, and how they shape workers' consciousness. Chapters 3 and 4 looked at the work processes and social relations of Macy's and Target, providing insight into the dynamics of leading department stores, while chapter 6 tackles the question of consciousness. But answering the question about change requires linking these two cases in a sequence and interrogating what they say about service evolution. This chapter does just that. Its more focused questions are whether sales work is being degraded and de-skilled or upgraded and enskilled and, if either of these, how we can we describe the regime toward which it is heading.

These questions come from labor process theory, the key concepts of which were outlined in chapter 1. There I discussed how Adam Smith and Karl Marx, though diverging in their interpretations, saw the transformation of craft into industrial labor as a routinization of tasks and increased control by employers. Twentieth-century theorists often saw opposite trends, such as shifts toward "post-industrial" employment (Bell 1973) or an upgrading of manufacturing with the advent of new technology (Blauner 1964). But Braverman (1974) returned the discussion to the models of Marx and Smith. While acknowledging that new occupations might, for a time, provide some workers challenging and autonomous roles, he saw the overarching tendency as "the worker [being] robbed of a craft heritage" and "given little or nothing to take its place" (5). Later thinkers (Burawoy 1979; Montgomery 1979; Edwards 1979) highlighted workers' resistance, which Edwards (1979, 179) saw engendering different managerial control strategies—simple, technical, and bureaucratic—that intersected with the secondary, "subordinate," and "independent primary" segments of the labor force. Others questioned whether there was any clear trajectory, earning the name "contingency" theorists since they posited "little net change in the skill requirements of work . . . or offsetting trends" (Spenner 1983, 825; Attewell 1987, 1990; Cockburn 1983; Penn 1986; Wood 1987). But despite these differing takes on skill change, agreement emerged that it could be broadly defined as complexity and autonomy and, in the sociological tradition, was best studied as an aspect of jobs rather than of individuals (Spenner 1983; Vallas 1987).

This chapter adapts this concept to frontline services and compares Macy's and Target as historical proxies for full-line and discount department stores. Though this approach has its limitations, there are also good reasons for viewing the two as sequential. For one, the Macy's stores I studied were some of the oldest in the company, and two out of three were unionized, thus more likely to retain past practices. For another, as seen in chapter 2, the growth of discounters has occurred against a proportional decline of full-line firms, indicating that the two are in competition with the former broadly winning. Finally, qualitative comparison of contemporary cases has long been used to assess historical change in industrial sociology (e.g., Blauner 1964; Edwards 1979; V. Smith 2001; Vallas 2003) and other fields of science.

Here I compare Macy's and Target across the three dimensions (organization, relations, and workers) discussed in chapter 1. I find that de-skilling is the clearest trajectory of emotional labor between the two, that this has been accompanied by a shift from adversarial to paternalist relations, and that this package of changes has been enabled by increased exploitation of secondary workers. I then return to Edwards's (1979) influential schema, arguing that none of his models fully describes these workplaces. Rather, Target displays a new model—"contingent control"—with Macy's, union and nonunion, showing transitional forms toward this. Conflicts and fissures are already evident in this regime, but workers' consciousness, examined in chapter 6, exposes deeper-seated tensions and inroads to organizing.

De-skilling Emotional Labor

Hochschild's (1983) "emotional labor" provides the starting point for most debates about service skill. Defined as "labor [that] requires one to induce or suppress feelings in order to sustain the outward countenance that produces the proper state of mind in others," it has been used to distinguish frontline services from manufacturing, clerical and other noninteractive jobs (7). Leidner (1999, 91) argues that emotional interaction turns workplace relations into "a three-way contest for control," while Sharon Bolton (2005) sees it as transcending workplace boundaries. Paul Brook (2009) and Jacques Bélanger and Paul Edwards (2013), however, think such claims are overblown. They argue that emotional labor, though a distinctive feature of service work, does not alleviate conflict between workers and managers but simply changes its form. They see services as subject to the same basic social forces as manufacturing and clerical work, which, often enough, have produced de-skilling (Crompton and Jones 1984). Is this what we see when we compare Macy's and Target?

At Macy's salespersons' roles were not uniform across the store; they varied with the type and price of product as well as with the ownership structure of departments (vendor-leased or Macy's-owned). A dividing line between commission and straight-hourly pay types separated high-end and low-end departments and salespeople, respectively. The tasks of all were multiple, however, including a greater number of maintenance and register duties previously performed by support staff. Multitasking, and the complexity inherent in that, was thus omnipresent.

But interactive selling was where emotional complexity was registered. All salespersons had an incentive to sell whether they received commission or not (because of the quota system) and to sell effectively, especially in high-priced, commission-based departments, often required extensive product knowledge that changed with the seasons, fashions, or product lines. A three-year Macy's salesman in men's suits reported that it took him "almost a year" to become familiar enough to sell effectively, and salespeople from other commissioned departments reported similar, elongated learning curves. Respondents from noncommissioned departments also emphasized the need for product knowledge in order to sell and meet their quotas; for example, one eleven-year saleswoman found "it's good to know the jeans so you can inform the customer on how the fit is." In several noncommissioned departments, however, knowledge and responsibility were placed more in the hands of specialists, with less expected of hourly associates than of their commission-earning counterparts.

But knowledge is only half the equation when it comes to selling. The other is persuasive ability. Macy's attempted to standardize this through MAGIC, but this method was less about reciting rote scripts and memorizing information (as at Target) than about engaging customers on a personal level, keeping them talking and through this process inducing them to buy—possibly more than they planned to. Customer interaction was inevitably varied given the personalities, wants, and means of customers. As a one-year specialist put it, "You can't come up to every customer the same way." "Improvising, it's really part of the job," said a first-year cosmetics saleswoman. Ken Bordieri, Local 1-S president and a former Macy's salesman remarked, "You have to keep your approach fresh—if you used the same spiel every time you would go out of your mind," or simply fail to sell. This kind of interaction that required practitioners "to be patient and observant with customers," (as a one-year specialist put it), to utilize aspects of their "basic socialized sel[ves]" (Bolton and Boyd 2003), and to apply specialized knowledge was closer to the deep acting performed by insurance or high-tech salespeople (Leidner 1993; Darr 2006) or luxury hotel attendants (Sherman 2007) than the routinized surface acting of fast-food or supermarket cashiers (Leidner 1993; Ritzer 1993; Tannock 2001; Tolich 1993). The unpredictability of customer emotions that required nuanced and varied responses from salespeople ensured them a degree of freedom from scripting, at least with regard to inputs. Sales output, as seen, was closely monitored.

At Target the situation was different. Salespersons were constantly beset with re-shop and zoning tasks while customer interaction was relegated to an interruption—albeit a prioritized one—of these functions. With the sole exception of those in electronics, who were expected to advise customers and sell "attachments," Target salespeople did not sell in the classic sense of proposing products and closing purchases. As a three-year salesman put it, "It is not a sales-based thing"; the first-year saleswoman and teacher described interaction as simply "being readily available to guests at any time they need something—that is going to make sales." Required product knowledge was thus considerably lower for Target than for Macy's salespersons. It was replaced, to some extent, with inventory and store-system knowledge: where items were, when they would be in stock, and how to find them. All tasks related to closing purchases, however, such as ringing up, processing payment, promoting the Target card, and customer surveys, were allocated to cashiers, whose separate roles were even more routinized.

If customer interaction required less product knowledge, and its average length and significance were reduced by the removal of final purchase, then it could already be seen as more predictable and hence less complex. But the complexity of emotional labor at Target was even further reduced by managerial scripting. "Can I help you find something?" was to be asked of all customers who came within ten feet, and use of this phrase was reinforced at daily huddles and one-on-one coaching sessions, as well as on the back of workers' company-supplied T-shirts. According to a two-year saleswoman, "Five-minute drills" were called "every half hour or hour [in which] everybody stops whatever they are doing and greets the guests with 'Can I help you find something?'" Parallel yet opposite to the open-ended complexity of Macy's interaction, the simplification and routinization of Target's interaction were combined with a reduction in salespersons' autonomy: they were told not only what to say but when and in which situations to say it. Such "prescriptive" emotion work (Bolton 2005) can more accurately be described as surface rather than deep acting, and it approximates the standardized expressions of fast-food servers and supermarket cashiers, as well as those of many call-center attendants (Leidner 1993; Tannock 2001; Tolich 1993; Taylor and Bain 1999).

Moving from Macy's to Target, keeping the salesperson at the center of our vision, we see a decline in both the complexity of her tasks and the autonomy granted to perform them. This is the de-skilling of emotional labor. It indicates that at least some corporate retailers are under the same imperative to routinize and control workers as their clerical and manufacturing counterparts. Skeptics might counter that full-line and discount stores occupy separate market segments and that it is segment-specific rather than overarching forces that lead the latter to de-skill and the former not to. If true, this would support contingency theory. But although the U.S. Census and National Retail Federation distinguish "full-line department" from "discount" (or "large-format value") stores, Macy's and Target cite each other as well as many other firms across this divide as "competitors" and "peers" in their own publications (Macy's 2012b, 2; Target 2012b, 13). The long-run trend of full-line firms has been "inexorable shrinking" since the rise of discounters, as seen in chapter 2, and firms in these two segments display clearly competitive relations, with discount stores winning (Spector 2005, 81). When asked whether there was any major difference between Macy's and Target shoppers, a first-year Target and former Macy's salesman replied, 'No, it's the same folks, looking for a good deal, looking for good customer service; there is really not a big difference.'

Moving from Macy's to Target—this time widening our vision to include support staff, stockers, and cashiers as well as salespersons—we also see increased collectivization. Sales at Macy's (union and nonunion), though supported by logistics and stock workers and the maintenance tasks of others, were carried out individually from customer contact to purchase. At Target, sales were accomplished collectively—and to a greater extent self-accomplished by customers—through the combined efforts of stock workers, cashiers, and salespersons. This whole process was aided by store design and the ubiquitous branding and advertising that have trained American consumers since the postwar era in what to expect in large, standardized stores (Cohen 2003). Furthermore, tasks were coordinated by computerized inventory and handheld devices (PDAs), cross-departmental communication (walkie-talkies), and store-level huddles. The de-skilling of salespersons from full-line to discount stores has thus also been accompanied by collectivization and mechanization, reminiscent of the transition from craft to assembly-line production in many manufacturing industries.

Collectivized selling at Target did require new abilities—what Ian Hampson and Anne Junor (2012, 526) refer to as "work process skills" and what David Harvey (2006, 109) foresaw as skills of "adaptability" that "entail literacy, numeracy, the ability to follow instructions and to routinize tasks quickly." These, however, are not the skills of a salesperson: they are the skills of operating and navigating the Target system or similar systems in other workplaces, much as the skills of a technician who programs smelting cycles in a modern steel plant are not those of a blacksmith but of an entirely different occupation. Moreover, adaptability and system knowledge—what some call "soft skills" (Nickson et al. 2012)—do not, at present, provide service workers means of securing their jobs and achieving advances in pay, security, or status. Instead, they may become the new baseline but not a source of leverage or empowerment.

The impacts of de-skilling and collectivization on worker-manager-customer relations were strangely convergent. At Macy's, customer interaction was more open-ended and had higher stakes than at Target, and workers were often socially distant from their customers, given Macy's more up-market orientation. Yet despite this, Macy's salespersons relied on customer cooperation, pursued personal conversations, and had material incentives to forgo managerial protocol in order to achieve sales. Management's quotas were a frequent source of tension that many felt inhibited their ability to properly serve customers. These dynamics pointed toward a latent worker-customer rather than worker-manager alliance at Macy's.

At Target, scripting and enforcement of "Can I help you find something?" combined with the requirement to interrupt maintenance tasks whenever customers asked produced resentment among salespersons toward both customers and managers. Many found customer questions and their disheveling of displays a nuisance. But worker-customer antagonism was not a prominent feature: the social proximity of the two groups at this more downmarket firm and the lower-stakes nature of their interactions—not having to end in sales to be successful—counteracted such tension. For cashiers, however, stakes were higher (because of checkout speed scores), and customer interaction was even more circumscribed and superficial. This engendered greater friction, with customers often seen by cashiers as obstacles to a speedy checkout. Altogether, the triangles of service and control at Macy's and Target, though distinct, did not produce radically different alliances.

Similarly, both firms made use of sex-typing. Salespersons were often placed in departments catering to same-sex customers, though it was in nonsales departments that more systematic segregation was evident. Target cashiers were overwhelmingly female, while stock and logistics workers were overwhelmingly male. At Macy's, a similar pattern was also evident. "Stock is mostly stock guys," said a ten-year saleswoman; "it's mostly guys that do the stock room. If it's ticketing and processing and stuff like that, we have a mixture of female and male, but if it's logistics, that is mostly guys." At Target, such differences involved a pay gap—a dollar more in starting wages for male-dominated logistics and electronics departments—and at Macy's there was evidence of this as well, though not as conclusive. Neither company differentially defined customer interaction for male and female workers, and both had gender-neutral service mottos (MAGIC and "Fast, Fun, Friendly). But women were placed in interactive positions more often than men, who were likely to be given noninteractive, manual jobs or sales positions requiring greater expertise that were also better paid.[1]

All of this suggests that even with the transformation of sales work from full-line to discount department stores—what I have called de-skilling—the age-old sex-typing of emotional labor as "feminine" has remained relatively constant.[2] This supports Milkman's (1987, 3) assertion that "once sex-typing takes root in an industry or occupation, it is extremely difficult to dislodge."

From Adversarialism to Paternalism

The most convincing trajectory of sales work in leading department stores is de-skilling, rather than contingency or upgrading. But changes in the structure of work are often accompanied by changes in the relations of employment—wages, benefits, managerial style, and the like. Here I show how the transformation of selling in the shift from full-line to discount stores has been not only accompanied but in fact enabled by a parallel shift from

1. There is a long history of big-ticket, commissioned sales jobs being both sex-typed and better paid for men than for women (see Jacoby 1997, 95–142).
2. See Moreton (2009) for an extended historical analysis of similar, if even more trenchant, sex-typing of interactive versus noninteractive jobs at Walmart.

adversarialism to paternalism, epitomized by Target's Disneyfied teamwork.

Macy's process was an eroded craft model in that it combined semiskilled selling with a broad-banding of tasks and a close monitoring of output. In this diminished state where workers had less autonomy than their mid-twentieth-century counterparts (chapter 2), elements of a germinal Taylorism could be discerned. Taylorism is a managerial method that involves subdivision and routinization of workers' tasks, as well as vigilant monitoring and attempts to raise their output. As such, it conflicts with most workers' preferences for a reasonable pace, predictable pay, and freedom from oversight. Frederick Taylor admitted that

> only about one man in eight was physically capable of handling 47½ tons per day [the amount he asked of lathe operators while a manager at Bethlehem Steel]. . . . The one man in eight who was able to do this work was in no sense superior to the other men who were working on the gang. He merely happened to be a man of the type of the ox . . . a man so stupid that he was unfitted to do most kinds of laboring work, even. (Quoted in Braverman 1974, 75)

This attitude, embodied in coordinated managerial experiments conducted across a number of firms in the 1910s and '20s, provoked understandable resistance (Edwards 1979; Montgomery 1987). Later iterations of the same approach, such as Fordism, have been seen to drive the rise of industrial unions in the 1930s and '40s and their particular "job control" practices (Lichtenstein 1982; O'Grady 1995). Through their very objectifying methods, Taylorism and its descendants thus played a pivotal role in spawning the "high-conflict/low-trust" paradigm of American industrial relations (Kochan, Katz, and McKersie 1994).

A similar dynamic was in place at the unionized Macy's stores I studied. There, a formal, adversarial culture reigned in which workers often distrusted managers. Local 1-S, despite its failures on the wage front, maintained a network of shop stewards that protected members from arbitrary discipline and dismissal. Their presence visibly conflicted with management's piecemeal attempts at teamwork, which were perceived by many as an effort "to confuse their associates by giving them recognition," as stated by a two-year salesman. At nonunion stores and with younger workers at unionized ones, managers sometimes used softer, human-relations approaches: holding daily meetings to recognize and motivate employees, rewarding them with "Macy's money" for goal attainment and good attendance, and engaging them in casual conversation. But contrary to these efforts, entry-level wages were just a notch above the legal minimum, benefits largely out of reach, and at nonunion stores, scheduling and job rotation were endemically erratic. Neither were managers at nonunion stores all supportive, as the experience of a five-year saleswoman made clear:

> Some of them [managers] need a lot more training. You really need to understand that everybody is not the same person, everybody is not robots. That is the whole thing: you have to treat people with respect. That is what is lacking amongst them; I think that is the biggest problem we have.

The uneasy coexistence of an adversarial culture with tentative teamwork initiatives defined Macy's employment relations.

Target, by contrast, was all about teamwork. It started this model in the early 1990s, when directors revamped employee relations with the help of Disney consultants, renaming customers "guests" and employees "team members" and instituting a host of new practices: huddles, the open-door policy, "great team member" cards, and the regular provision of food and entertainment, as well as the "one team, one dream" and "fast, fun, friendly" mottos (Rowley 2003). In chapter 3 I labeled Target's flexible, just-in-time sales process service Toyotism after the analogous methods of Japanese automakers (Dohse, Jürgens, and Malsch 1985). And Toyotist processes are often seen alongside softer managerial practices than those found in Taylorist or Fordist workplaces. Taylor himself, if not all of his followers, recognized a disjunction between the interests of workers and management; human resource management (HRM), by contrast, typically denies such conflict and advances instead a unitary theory of workplace interest. Critics of HRM describe it as coaxing workers to give more for less money while preventing unionization. Some teamwork advocates even support this characterization, such as the auto plant manager who responded to a researcher that "everything I do and breathe is designed to prevent a union from coming in here!" (Milkman 1991, 104).

At Target I found strong evidence of similar goals. Alongside its teamwork ethos the company pursued robust union prevention, which, in its film adaptation, referred explicitly to this mantra. Another claim was that unionization would "hurt our store's ability to serve guests" by decreasing workers' flexibility: "If the unions tried to organize Target," states the white male actor, "they could also try to bring along their way of doing business—an old-fashioned, rigid structure." Here the company's strategy departed doubly from adversarialism: first, by denying conflict of interest and second, by not rigidly binding workers to particular roles.

Target's labor process would have been hard to implement in a unionized store or a more specialized, up-market one. The company's nonunion history[3] and down-market orientation enabled these developments, much as the frailty of Japanese unions in the postwar era enabled the development of lean manufacturing there (Moody 1997, 85). At the same time, Target's system did not require union absence: a union could allow for flexible role allocation, could support the "friendly" attitude of salespersons, etc. But it would necessarily encroach on management's power to do such allocating, as well as scheduling, promoting, and giving raises. This hypothetical difference was actually observed between union and nonunion Macy's. Union-sponsored wage gains would also encroach on profits, but the impact of this in firms such as Target, Macy's, or Walmart is estimated to be small even if this were an important consideration.[4]

Edwards (1979) as well as Montgomery (1979) and Burawoy (1979) argue that de-skilling can be resisted by workers or enabled by managerial overtures. Both were found at the stores I studied. Because of union resistance and Macy's up-market orientation, its ability to standardize and routinize selling was more

3. During the biggest wave of department store organizing in the 1930s, managers at J.L. Hudson's (later part of Dayton-Hudson) flagship store in Detroit successfully fended off unionization through extensive use of guards and premium pay for nonstrikers (Kirstein 1950, 65–66). Not until 1990 was a union (United Auto Workers [UAW] Local 3500) certified by the NLRB at a Westland, Michigan, Hudson's store (then part of Dayton-Hudson), which, because of the company's legal challenges, did not obtain a first contract until 1998. In 2004 the store was part of a general sell-off by then-renamed Target Corporation of its department store division to Federated, which later became Macy's, Inc.

4. Catherine Reutschlin (2012) estimates that raising the wage floor for all workers at U.S. retail firms with one thousand or more employees (1,300 firms, five million workers) by 27 percent (from $9.10 to $12.25 per hour) would result in additional annual costs of $20.8 billion; the annual profits of those same firms likely surpassed $70 billion in 2012, not counting the billions more ($24 billion in 2011 for just the top ten retailers) used to pay for "stock buybacks."

limited than that of downscale Target, its "cheap chic" image notwithstanding. In parallel but reverse fashion, Target's development of a flexibly routinized system was externally aided by its discount focus and union absence yet internally maintained by a deceptively "flat" hierarchy and proactive paternalism. The deskilling of emotional labor found here is therefore not the result of some inexorable process. It is the outcome of struggles between workers and managers, other companies' learning from these, and companies' interaction with their market environment over an extended period of time.

Deflating Expectations

It also matters who fills the jobs management designs. As discussed in chapter 4, there were key differences between Macy's and Target's workers. These were not merely happenstance, a by-product of differing regimes, but were instead an integral part of the shift from the adversarial, eroded craft model to the paternalist, service Toyotist one. One result of such shifts was lowered expectations, which can translate into muted opposition and class consciousness.

Macy's workers, union or nonunion, were divided. On the one hand, there were many middle-aged, full-time employees who typically worked in higher-priced or commission-based departments, who had been at Macy's for years, and whose wages were their primary source of income. Then there was a larger group of younger, often part-time and more transient workers, typically in lower-priced departments, whose Macy's wages were secondary to their basic needs. Although age was a major feature of this distinction, race, nativity, and gender were not. Why did such division exist at Macy's?

Despite attempts by management to lower full-time hours, Local 1-S had maintained them at 37.5 per week in the stores it represented. After three months' employment, all members were protected from arbitrary dismissal and after five years from lay-off. Because of this, some unionized workers stayed at Macy's long enough to see considerable raises, such as the thirty-one-year salesman who earned $22.75; commissioned-based wages entered this range earlier and could potentially climb higher, even at nonunion stores. These Macy's workers could more often support themselves without public assistance or family help. The flip side, of course, was an expanding low-skill, low-wage, and often part-time sector of the sales force that was largely filled by younger, secondary workers. This lower tier was made possible by the simplification of sales and greater self-service in down-market departments. But although it had grown, the size of this group was limited insofar as Macy's needed up-market, service-centered departments to distinguish it from discounters.

Target, again, was different. Instead of dualism, it had a workforce in which young and secondary workers were the vast majority, with older, primary workers relegated to a small minority. Of the eleven Target respondents who did not have major family support, none were without some external income. For five this was public assistance (Social Security income, public or state-subsidized housing, Medicaid), for two it was an equivalent-earning spouse, for three it was a combined household with extended family members, and for one it was a second job. This was in contrast to Macy's, where most primary-earning respondents could provide for themselves without such assistance.[5] But low-wage workers at

5. They were all single adults with no children or other dependents.

both firms often depended on government programs to afford necessities like housing, health care, and food. At the national level this same situation has been widely interpreted as a public cost and subsidy for low-wage employers (Jacobs, Perry, and MacGillvary 2015).

Target's streamlined stores required fewer trained salespersons and, because there was no union, granted workers scant security and few prospects for raises. These features disincentivized Target jobs for anyone seeking sustainable work. And Target seemed to know this: many respondents noted how managers allowed student employees to work around class schedules and take time off for exams. Several thought management deliberately hired students, a view supported by the "college students" page on the "careers" section of Target's website, complete with video testimonials from student employees (Target Corporation 2013). Whether the company purposely hired immigrants or the children of immigrants was harder to determine, but by its own admission and the reports of respondents, it pursued more systematic referral hiring than Macy's. In an immigrant-rich city where people of Caribbean origin are the largest single group, it was perhaps unsurprising that Target's New York stores had higher proportions of both.

Moving from Macy's to Target, we see increased exploitation of young, non-primary workers—a pattern also noted by Guy Standing (2011) and Arne Kalleberg (2011) with parallels in the early history of industrialization (Dublin 1979). Secondary workers, by definition, have less to lose by quitting and often lower expectations of any given job, making them more likely to exit bad jobs than to voice opposition and possibly make them better (Hirschman 1970). But whether retailers' attempts to deflate expectations through demographic shifts have had their intended effects can be assessed only in the next chapter.

An Outline of Contingent Control

Comparing Macy's and Target as representatives of full-line and discount department stores, I identified differences that I argued were moments in a trend toward a regime like Target's. But what *is* that regime? Chapter 3 defined Macy's process as eroded craft and Target's as service Toyotism, while chapter 4 examined employment relations and worker characteristics at each firm. This chapter has thus far argued for a connection between elements, such that each case—unionized Macy's, nonunion Macy's, and Target—coheres as a system of labor control.[6] None of these systems faced major internal disruption at the time of study (though the two unionized Macy's came close in June 2011), nor were they failing to produce enough revenue or replenish their workforces in the face of rapid turnover. How were they able to sustain themselves, given the meager wages, benefits, and security they offered?

Writing in the late 1970s before the full onslaught of deunionization, Richard Edwards (1979) formulated a three-part schema of workplace control consisting of simple, technical, and bureaucratic forms. The purpose of this model was to explain not only the historical evolution of workplace systems in the United States but also the divided structure of the U.S. working class and the chances for transformative action. Much has changed since 1979, however. The subordinate primary group that Edwards equated with unionized mass-production workers has been reduced from a mainstay to an anomaly. The independent primary group of

6. To call something a "system" or a "regime" is not to imply that its dynamics are somehow predetermined, necessary, or morally justified. Any system can become chaotic or inefficient or require actions that are morally reprehensible. The point, however, is that all three sets of stores continue to exist and function in general agreement with their corporations' goals.

managers and professionals in bureaucratic settings has expanded somewhat, but the guarantees and stability they once enjoyed have been eroded (Ehrenreich and Ehrenreich 2013). Finally, the heterogeneous secondary category filled by "simpl[y]" controlled and typically non-union small goods producers," "service," "retail," and "temporary . . . office work[ers]" (Edwards 1979, 179) has either nearly disappeared (in the first case) or greatly expanded (in the latter three), with frontline services increasingly organized, not by small proprietors but by large corporations such as Walmart, McDonald's, and Yum! Brands, as well as Macy's and Target (Ritzer 1993; Schlosser 2001; Lichtenstein 2009). "Simple control," understood as an informal, entrepreneurial form of work organization, can hardly be said to characterize the work systems of large service bureaucracies. "Technical control," understood as the assembly-line paradigm, describes aspects of contemporary services, particularly at firms like Target, but their degree of collectivization and mechanization are still far from those of Fordism. And although service corporations are undoubtedly "bureaucratic," key features of that regime—living wages, job security, and internal labor markets—were absent at the stores I studied.

This raises the question, Do the modes of control at Macy's and Target represent new, as yet undertheorized regimes? If so, what are their defining features? I argue they embody a regime of contingent control that extends beyond Edwards's three types. Target's model was more coherent, likely more representative of contemporary service employers and thus ideal-typical; Macy's union and nonunion models were imperfect versions—workplaces in transition from the simple control of mid-twentieth-century department stores to the contingent control of twenty-first-century discounters.

Contingent Employment

The primary feature of contingent control is the contingent nature of employment for most workers. The Bureau of Labor Statistics defines "contingent workers" as "those who do not have an implicit or explicit contract for ongoing employment"; 5.7 million workers, or 4.1 percent of the U.S. workforce, fell into this group in the most recent survey (U.S. Bureau of Labor Statistics 2005). But scholars have noted the spread of other employment types that deviate from the mid-twentieth-century standard of an indefinite contract and full-time hours (Tilly 1996; V. Smith 1998; Kalleberg 2011). This broader category of "part-time, temporary and contract work" (Kalleberg 2000) has been referred to as "nonstandard" by some, "precarious" by others (Fudge and Owens 2006; Standing 2011), but the common feature of these arrangements is that workers are easily expendable. They are hence contingent—not necessary—to the ongoing operation of a firm, and I use this term to indicate all part-time, temporary, and other nonstandard employment relationships.

Contingency as just defined can be produced in several ways. First, it can be embodied in actual employment contracts. During holidays and peak shopping seasons Macy's and Target each hired sizable numbers of seasonal staff whose terms of employment were ninety days or less; Macy's also employed "on-call" workers who had no guaranteed hours and, like their seasonal counterparts, could not become members of Local 1-S. This strict form of contingency, however, included only a minority of workers at each firm.

A second form of contingency is produced by erratic scheduling, even for indefinitely employed staff. At unionized Macy's there were three categories of employment—full-time, part-time, and short-hour—each with minimum weekly hours (37.5, 20, and 12 hours, respectively). Despite management's attempt to reduce full-time hours, Local 1-S had upheld them, as well as the minimums for part-time and short-hour positions, thus limiting the expansion of contingency among its membership. Target, by contrast, provided no guaranteed hours to anyone below specialists: weekly hours for team members, the vast majority, fluctuated from forty or more during high seasons to twenty or less during low ones, though individual variation was tied to performance and in some cases, personal relations with supervisors.

A third form of contingency comes from the outright denial of job security. Because of Local 1-S, all Macy's workers employed for ninety days or more had rights to due process before dismissal and an appeal process afterward; after five years they were also protected from layoffs. Target workers had no such rights: they could be dismissed at any time by supervisors and had no feasible appeals process. Managers' freedom to determine workers' schedules at both firms, however, presented another way of decreasing job security. At Target team leaders and ETLs sometimes used inconvenient scheduling combined with overall hour reduction to "manage out" individual employees. Though Macy's managers were unable to reduce workers' overall hours, their freedom to set shifts made possible similar separation strategies.

The advantages for employers of a predominantly contingent workforce consist in power, savings, and flexibility: power insofar as marginally attached, expendable employees are less likely or able to question managerial authority; costs insofar as their pay and benefits are lower ; and flexibility insofar as they can be hired and fired (or scheduled/not scheduled) to fit fluctuating demand—a feature more prominent in services than in durable goods manufacturing. Low pay and benefits, combined with few chances for promotion, also produce a fourth form of contingency: when material rewards are unsustainable for primary workers, many will leave in search of better pay, creating high turnover. At both Macy's and Target turnover was high (though not as uniformly at Macy's) and on par with that of other service firms, such as McDonald's (Leidner 1993; Tannock 2001) and Walmart (Lichtenstein 2009; Moreton 2009).

Contingent employment is thus the defining feature of contingent control. It was more pronounced at Target than at Macy's, though contingency was on the rise there too. Why doesn't such extensive contingency impede firms' ability to function? Comparison of Macy's and Target shows that three features are pivotal: standardized work, a benevolent bureaucracy, and a pliant workforce.

Standardized Work

Contingent employment implies high turnover. If tasks are specialized and require training to do properly, this decreases workers' expendability and hence the guiding purpose of contingency. In manufacturing, standardization was fully achieved only on the basis of mass production for mass markets, which in turn had to be actively supported by government policy, advertising, and new consumption norms (Aglietta 1979; Sabel 1982; Leach 1993). The creation of such markets in the mid-twentieth century provided necessary but not sufficient conditions for the standardization of customer service. The immediate postwar decades saw continued expansion of high-service department stores and the rise of high-service specialty chains, alongside the burgeoning discount phenomenon (Cohen 2003; Zukin 2004). It was only in the 1970s and '80s that self-service shopping became a predominant mode of consumption, at which time firms in this sector were considerably less concentrated than they are today (Bluestone et al. 1981; Lichtenstein 2009). At present, just a handful of companies—Walmart, Costco, Target, and the Kmart division of Sears Holdings—dominate the discount arena, and the last of these is clearly in decline. Economies of scale and consumer acceptance of discounters thus provided the sufficient conditions for standardized selling, and these are relatively recent developments.

Discount retail and services generally, unlike their midrange and upscale counterparts, are more susceptible to standardization since price and dependability rather than service and variety are the main selling points. Target, for example, has been able to effect greater standardization of its offerings than Macy's because of its lowered emphasis on brand and fashion and greater focus on household products (small appliances, cleaning supplies, etc.) that are less varied than, for example, sweaters or cologne. Because its offerings were standardized, Target was less reliant on skilled salespersons, who were almost completely absent. But decreased reliance on skill and knowledge did not itself standardize tasks: stocking, maintenance, and service duties were actively routinized by management, and workers' adherence to these prescriptions was daily reinforced at huddles, in planograms, in one-on-one talks with supervisors, and on register and PDA screens.

Macy's, for its part, attempted to standardize offerings and maintenance as much as possible in lower-tier departments while pursuing a half-hearted routinization of customer service through its MAGIC sales method. Yet it still needed skilled salespersons to move products in high-tier departments since only they could advise customers about highly varied merchandise and persuade them to buy costly, semiluxury items. Even in low-tier, noncommissioned departments, Macy's often depended on salespersons' individual initiative. Despite seeming simplicity, open-ended interactions that had to end in a purchase required more of all Macy's salespersons than the generic and low-stakes helpfulness expected of Target workers.

The more work is standardized, the more expendable workers become, and the more companies can rely on contingent rather than long-term employees. Macy's and Target had both traveled far on this vector, but Target, because of its downscale focus and proactive union prevention, had traveled further. It could therefore make greater use of contingent labor.

The Benevolent Bureaucracy

Standardization implies tighter managerial control, which is not an easy pill to swallow. Combined with low wages, benefits, and security, standardization can engender frustration and opposition among workers. In service workplaces where deference to customers and positive displays of feeling are required, such resentment can negatively impact sales. Thus if contingency reduces the costs and demands of workers, and standardization enables this, what then are the shop-floor relations that minimize friction? Here Target's paternalism came to the fore: it offered bad jobs but good managers, while Macy's offered a few good jobs (though mostly bad) and harsher oversight.

Target presented itself as a company that cared. Although it paid workers little, provided no guaranteed hours or job security and few affordable benefits, many interviewees—more than at Macy's—had favorable views of the company. Reports such as "this is a great job, this is a great store" (from a one-year salesman); "I think Target is a good place because we have people to talk to, counselors, if anything is going on at home" (from a first-year saleswoman); or, "I think it is a fun place to work because everybody is cool and relaxed—they are people you can go to as a friend, even the managers" (from a two-year salesman) were not uncommon. Target's human-relations techniques—team building, open-door policy, informal style, and low-cost welfarism—combined with the absence of an organized counterweight, contributed greatly to such positive perceptions.

But another aspect was also crucial: daily communication of sales volatility and implication of these in workers' schedules. "If we are consistently not making sales goals," related Amy, the first-year saleswoman and teacher, "then *we* are going to be short on giving people hours and pay because if we aren't making their goals *we* can't pay" (emphasis added). A one-year in-stock worker similarly believed that "Target cannot do anything; it is the guests who decide with their strength the profitability or success of Target." Neither individual was a manager, stockholder, or in any way empowered to make decisions about pay and schedules. Yet Amy identified with management and despite being an active union member at her other job—where she struggled against layoff and benefit reduction—accepted Target's claims that pay and hours had to follow sales. The second worker, a recent West African immigrant, accepted this logic as well, and neither he nor Amy was alone in that view. Target had thus done much to integrate workers into its goals and outsource blame for contingency onto "the market."

Macy's, by contrast, pursued an "extreme individualization of the sales effort," in Ken Bordieri's words, that placed responsibility for sales on individual workers rather than market conditions. Management, particularly at nonunion stores, used aspects of HRM, including rallies, recognition cards, prizes and rewards (Macy's money), and a piecemeal informal style. But Local 1-S and its shop-stewards were visible counterweights to this in union-ized stores, and even in nonunion ones formality and condescen-sion prevailed. Furthermore, by individualizing sales Macy's was unable to externalize blame for shifting hours and pay. Workers were left either to blame themselves—perhaps inflicting "hidden injuries of class" (Sennett and Cobb 1972)—or to blame manag-ers and by proxy the company. Neither was conducive to a cheery morale.

HRM techniques, when pursued systematically as at Target, can dull the conflict embedded in standardized, contingent work regimes. They are also useful for promoting positive and deferen-tial attitudes among service workers. Yet some workers are more receptive than others to such overtures, and these factors further grease the wheels of contingent control.

A Pliant Workforce

Macy's, as we saw, had a dual workforce, while Target had an overwhelmingly young and secondary one with a few older, pri-mary workers mixed in. At both firms primary workers typically had higher expectations for pay and benefits, as well as for digni-fied treatment from management. It was among them that both firms' attempts at team building were least effective. "A lot of them speak to you like a child," said a two-year Target cashier and single mother. "I am an adult with my own kids. I don't even talk to my kids the way they talk to me."

Consensus-building is inevitably more effective when work-ers are predisposed to accept it. Although age, gender, and labor-market status are not identical with such predispositions, at both Macy's and Target younger, secondary workers typically had lower, short-term hopes for their jobs than older, primary workers. In the next chapter I will show they also evinced less opposition to managers and were less often prounion, implying greater receptivity to teamwork. The degree to which employers can recruit secondary workers, therefore, increases their chances for successful team building through HRM and limits potential resistance.

Target, I found, hired more college students and college-aged individuals than Macy's. It offered flexible, part-time hours that students could adjust to class schedules, as well as a premium entry-level wage. Although $9.50 per hour (or $10.50 for stock and electronics workers) was well below the cost of living in New York, it was higher than the wages for many other entry-level jobs, including those at Macy's. Target's more systematic referral hiring also allowed it access to broader networks of similar job seekers.

Macy's hiring, as well as other aspects of its managerial practice, were slowly converging toward those of Target. This was seen in the increased hiring of young workers on "flexible" schedules in nonunion stores, as well as similar shifts within the low-tier departments of unionized stores. But again, the extent to which this was possible was limited by Macy's up-market orientation, requiring it to maintain specialized—and typically older—employees in its commission-based, higher-priced departments. And these workers were less likely to accept teamwork overtures. Contingent control, in its robust form, encounters fewer obstacles at downscale firms like Target than at midmarket ones like Macy's.

Internal Tensions

There are two contradictions inherent in contingent control. One is in the workplace, and the other is between it and the wider economy. In workplaces defined by this regime the contingent nature of employment clashes with the benevolent style of management—bad jobs but good managers. Unstable, low-wage jobs traditionally found among "simply" controlled workplaces (using Edwards's framework) are combined with low-cost versions of the welfarism once found among large, nonunion bureaucracies (Jacoby 1997). Target, and Macy's to a lesser extent, provided free food and discounts, but not living wages and benefits. Neither did they provide meaningful pathways to advancement: managers at both firms were recruited mostly from outside the sales force and were required to have a bachelor's degree. Managerial care, teamwork, friendliness, and so forth thus failed to align with most workers' concrete conditions.

The second tension of contingent control is between the firms that practice it and the environment in which they operate. Given the long-term excess of undertrained, underemployed workers in the United States and the profit motives of most employers, it makes sense for each company to reduce its labor costs and labor demands by increasing contingency. But when enough employers follow suit, this decreases the overall quality of jobs and effective demand in the economy. When more and more primary workers are forced to take secondary-type jobs, the gulf between expectations and reality becomes wider, heightening the precariousness of contingent regimes.

Some might question the utility of contingent control as a concept, asking whether a series of discrete processes might do the same trick. In recent years many fine-grained studies (e.g., Kalleberg 2011) have described the phenomena and causes of "nonstandard" work, while Standing (2011) has done the opposite, elevating contingent or "precarious" workers into a new general category meant to replace the "proletariat" of old. The problem with empiricist, discrete approaches is that they miss the forest for the trees: they identify varieties of contingent work but fail to link these to concrete work processes and the institutional forms that use them. Standing's approach similarly ignores the relative autonomy of the labor process but from an aerial viewpoint that implausibly merges forests and meadows, or in his case freelancers and day laborers, into a single group. Contingent control is more ambitious than the first and more restrained than the second. It captures the emerging practices of large, for-profit bureaucracies, how these are related to increasing standardization and to burgeoning secondary workforces. Because it sees the workplace as a semiautonomous moment within the larger economy, it can pinpoint its internal and external contradictions. The next chapter probes workers' experience of these tensions and their willingness to challenge them.

6

Class Consciousness on the Sales Floor

Deborah had worked at Macy's for ten years and was earning $11 an hour when we spoke. I asked if she identified with her work. "We start to get passionate about the job," she replied. "It's like being a chef, you want to make the most fantastic dish, you want to look out and see the customer enjoying the dinner." Deborah's feelings toward coworkers were not so positive. "It's very hard, it's hostile," she said. "It's like you are working on commission but you're not—that's how Macy's becomes since they introduced the [sales] metrics." But Deborah did not fault managers or the company. "I love Macy's, from my heart!" she told me.

David had worked at Macy's for three years and at slightly better pay. "When new suits come in," he stated, "I take a look at the material they are made of, how they fit, because you want to know how to explain it to customers. I want to be knowledgeable." Though he did not see retail as a career, David was more invested in his job than the typical stopgap worker (Tannock 2001). Like Deborah, he felt little connection with coworkers: "It's more competition than I would like. I have gotten into arguments with other workers." But unlike Deborah, he was skeptical of managers. "They want to keep that distance between manager and sales associate," he said. "I don't agree with that personally, that they are on a pedestal."

Vanessa's views were perhaps more expected of young, short-term workers. A college student at the time, she had worked at Target for a little under a year. "In five years," she told me, "I want to be a social worker; I don't want to be at Target then, it's just not what I want to do." Unlike Deborah and David, Vanessa liked her coworkers: "Target to me is like one big old family. Everyone talks and there are a lot of friendships." She also felt close to managers: "The relationship is friendly, comfortable, they don't make you feel not comfortable. You just do the work and there won't be any problems."

Derek had a somewhat different take. Like Vanessa, he didn't much identify with his job. "I'm not even aiming to be at Target next year," he told me. "I want to go back to school and study psychology." Also like Vanessa, Derek felt close with many coworkers: "Most get along with each other perfectly fine. If you don't become friends here, you were probably friends beforehand." But he saw managers as hostile: "The model of the store is 'fast, fun, and friendly' but the whole friendly situation doesn't work out that well. . . . It's a confusing state and sometimes things get a little out of hand."

These snapshots into workers' lives expose divergent and unexpected views. Many, mostly at Macy's, expressed some form of job identity but did not see their interests in line with other workers'. Some, like Deborah, identified with their jobs but did not fault management for their degradation and low pay. Others, who, like David, shared job identity and a lack of solidarity, resented managers' approach. Vanessa and Derek—and many of their Target peers—had little job identity but strong bonds with their coworkers. Yet while Vanessa saw managers as part of "one big family," Derek did not even find them "friendly." What was the overall pattern of these views? Were they related in any way to Macy's and

Target's work regimes? Or did they result purely from workers' experience outside the workplace?

These questions go to the heart of this book. I interrogate them here using the dimensions of class consciousness outlined in chapter 1—occupational identity, coworker solidarity, and management opposition as well as union support. Clear differences emerged between Macy's and Target workers on these scores. But when I asked about their social and political views outside the workplace, these differences disappeared, leaving a generalized picture of frustration and distrust. I consider these perspectives in a fifth section before taking stock of the impact of work, employment relations, and workers' life positions.

Identity

Identity with one's occupation has long been a source of collectivism and union activism, particularly along craft as opposed to industrial lines (Brody 1964; [1964] Preis 1972; Montgomery 1979; Cobble 1991a). It implies recognition of one's role in production and can provide inroads to class consciousness. Of the workers I interviewed, none had dreamed of becoming a salesperson, or cashier or stock clerk. But many took pride in their abilities, their product knowledge, and their understanding of sales. Some even claimed to have "trained" their managers.

Most Macy's respondents voiced such opinions. A four-year saleswoman stated, "I'm really good at what I do: I make my goals, I make my credits, I interact with customers, because that's naturally me; it's nothing I have to work at." A first-year salesman found that "retail helps your people skills and I think that helps you inside for who you are; it makes you help people." "I just fell in love with retail," said a two-year saleswoman. "I like working with people,

I love Macy's, I love the tourists, I love the merchandise, it's never boring." A one-year salesman in his midtwenties had "been working in retail since [he] was eighteen," but when I asked if he would stay there he was more ambiguous:

> It depends. There's a guy who works in my store [department] as an actor and he's approaching thirty and the only reason he deals with it [retail] is because of the flexibility that you don't get with an office job. For a lot of artists and people who are really starving for something else, I think retail complements them.

Among older, long-term Macy's workers who had fewer alternative prospects, occupational identity was high. "It's been rewarding for me helping a lot of people here," said a two-year specialist in her sixties. "It's a really good feeling." But they were also quick to voice complaints: "I never want to see another retail job again in my life," she continued, "not in this lifetime. I'm waiting until I get my Social Security and I'm gonna run!" A four-year saleswoman in her forties found that "as you [get] into working retail you see different aspects. For me, I could see it as a life going on." And a ten-year specialist stated that she and her coworkers had "one common goal: satisfying customers. You feel good satisfying customers, when they leave the store knowing that they got what they wanted."

Younger, short-term workers had less attachment to their jobs. A two-year support worker advised, "Don't look into making it a career—you didn't go to school for this." A first-year cosmetics saleswoman, when asked whether she saw retail as a career, responded, "Definitely not. It's more of a college thing, but it doesn't pay, I can't do that forever." Another saleswoman in the same department said, "I'm just working for Metro card money because I go to school. I want to go into my field; I don't want to be doing this." The first, however, believed her job was "a good experience for when I actually go to beauty school," and the second enjoyed it: "We like cosmetics; before I came to Macy's I knew a lot about the products. We all share the same passion." But another saleswoman in her twenties, although she had studied fashion, saw little of herself in her job: "I graduated in July and I really don't want to do design anymore. I don't know what I want to do with my life so I just took some time off and I needed work to support myself. I just got the first job that hired me."

Unlike their peers at Target, several short-term Macy's workers took pride in their work. David, the three-year suit salesman encountered earlier, described his attainment of product knowledge, noting that "not everybody does this, some salespeople just stick to their area, [but] I try to know the whole suit area." A younger two-year salesman in women's shoes stated, "When I first started the job was a challenge—I learned how to be customer savvy. This job pushed me to that limit because if you don't get a customer to like you, how are you going to sell? I am not going to leave this job until I am completely done with retail." And a two-year saleswoman, also in men's suits, described her growing respect for selling:

> The only thing I came here with was that I like men's [clothing]. My background in journalism allows me to learn things. Little details like shirt sleeves—I just didn't see it [before]. When I came in here I would have to do a measurement but now I could size you just by looking at you. I would say you are a 38 shirt length, a 32 waist, 32 length.

Her guess was largely accurate. In commissioned departments like these, salespersons had more product knowledge and were under greater pressure to sell than their non-commissioned colleagues. They were therefore more often personally invested in their jobs, even if their long-term goals lay elsewhere.

At Target, statements of identity with work were few and far between. Of the five who expressed such views, four were middle-aged adults without college degrees, and the fifth was an electronics salesman who hoped to become a manager. All others saw themselves outside Target and outside retail in the long term. "I give myself another year," said a two-year cashier, "and if I stay that long it's gonna be part-time for extra cash. I couldn't see myself working at Target as a cashier all my life." "Where do you see yourself in five years?" I asked a first-year saleswoman.

> *A:* Photography, I want to have my own photography business, that's what I went to school for.
>
> *Q:* So you don't want to stay at Target long-term?
>
> *A:* No, no I don't. I want to start my own stuff, I don't want to work for nobody else. I don't mind working here but some days in my head I say, "No, I am not coming back."

"So you don't want to make retail a career?" I asked a one-year saleswoman in her twenties. She answered,

> Hell no! Excuse my language—hell no! No no no no no. That's what they [managers] expect, that you are going to stay here forever, they think that you can't get any other job nowhere else and you will stay here forever, but no that is not the case.

Though most were not as negative, they similarly lacked enthusiasm for their work. A common refrain was that Target was good for now. "I see Target as a form of springboard," said a one-year stock worker. "Retail is a good place to start life, not to be forever." "It's not like I'm saying it's a bad environment," explained a first-year saleswoman. "It's great. I'm just saying it's not my career, so when I'm done with school I'm gonna find a new job." A first-year salesman and former Macy's worker said his plans to move on had "nothing to do with managers or pay, it's just me personally and what I see for myself. I feel like I would be settling with Target and that is not something I want to settle for."

Many, however, did cite pay as a reason. "I would rather work someplace else that pays differently but not at Target and not at this pay," said a first-year saleswoman. A one-year stock worker commented, "It's not the way I want to live—it's a job where you make less than fifteen grand a year." But a more common reason was boredom. "They haven't really taught me anything new here," said the first-year salesman and former Macy's employee. "It's mostly common sense: if you have common sense you can work in retail." Another first-year salesman expressed similar dissatisfaction:

A: A career is something you can enjoy, something that you don't wake up every morning and think "I want to quit" or you are always looking for something else—that's what I think of as a job, something you do just to get money.

Q: And what do you think of Target as?

A: It's a job. It felt like a career at first but now it feels like a job.

A four-year salesman got "bored real fast, so I don't want to stay here forever. I look at the managers and their jobs are even more boring than ours; it's pretty routine." And a two-year cashier found "standing all day in the same spot . . . aggravating. I like to move around and do stuff. Any chance I get I take to do bags or customer service just so I can move around."

Target jobs provided few chances to problem solve or think creatively. Those who found ways to do so were either in electronics—where selling was more skilled—or enjoyed customer interaction. A two-year electronics salesman "tr[ied] to acknowledge myself with as much information as I can. I do have customers that come in thinking we are supposed to know everything about our merchandise, so I try to read as much information as I can about it." His plans in five years were to "probably [still] be in school. And if I get promoted, yeah, I will be at Target. I think it is a fun place to work." The seven-year saleswoman and former garment worker emphasized her service skills: "Sometimes you have to go out of your way to please them. But you [also] have to know what you are talking about. I enjoy what I do," she continued, "because if I didn't I would've switched to another department a long time ago."

These views were a distinct minority at Target. Differences in job identity between Macy's and Target workers could partly be traced to age and job tenure, but disparities also existed between young, short-term workers at both firms. Among them, the more engaging nature of Macy's sales jobs seemed to make the difference.

Solidarity

If occupational identity is a part of class identity that can be formed in the workplace, coworker solidarity, defined as affinity and common interest, is another. The patterning of these views was the reverse of job identity: only a minority at Macy's showed clear solidarity with their coworkers, compared with a large majority at Target. Unionization made little clear difference, though it contributed to Macy's two-tier benefit structure, which engendered some resentment among newer workers.

"I work in dresses," said a first-year Macy's saleswoman in her twenties. "It is mostly older women [who work there] and they are very competitive—I've seen them argue with each other in front of customers." "Is it competitive?" I asked a two-year saleswoman about her relationship with coworkers. "It is," she replied. "People are always watching your numbers. Even with friends, at the end of the day you will fight to pull out those last statistics." A seven-year salesman felt "there's this competition between associates where it's like they gotta get their goal and it's totally killed the morale; it really has pitted worker against worker." "Even if we did go on strike," said a two-year stock worker about the events of 2011, "I still would've went to work." When I asked if he was concerned about attempted hour reductions for full-timers he replied, "The main people it would've affected were people who have been here for fifteen or twenty years"—not him.

These statements emphasize competition over common interest. They came more frequently from Macy's workers, union and nonunion alike. The company's quota system was often a source of friction. "Part-timers don't really work with the full-timers," remarked a first-year saleswoman, "because we have our own separate goals, and if we work with them they are going to get the sale." "They are fighting now over there," said a thirty-one-year salesman as we spoke at a nearby café. "She was supposed to be on this side, he was over there, and they didn't make the goal, so let them ring [up customers], what's the big deal? But they [managers] do that on purpose, for me and you to fight, that's what they want. . . . It's an unfair system." But friction also came from age and ethnic differences. A first-year specialist told me, "I'm from Trinidad. Here are a lot of African Americans, a lot of Spanish [Hispanic] people. Some of the African American people don't speak to the Spanish people, but guess what? I'm the middle person—they both talk to me." A salesman in his twenties found "there are some older associates you can relate to, but the younger ones I have more of a connection with," while a stock worker in her twenties had "not so much" in common with her coworkers: "Most of them are married with kids and I think this is what they do." And a two-year saleswoman who later claimed "a feeling of solidarity" described her initial exclusion:

> At the beginning I took some hazing and I don't know whether it was because I was a temp or because I was white. I lived in a cul-de-sac in Georgia—It was so white where I lived. All I knew was if I wanted to earn respect I had to work my ass off. And that's what I did. Now they call me sister and I don't feel I'm treated any differently.

Though racial tensions were rarely mentioned—and often minimized—those based on age and tenure came up often.

Not all Macy's workers were without fellow feeling, however. "Even when Macy's doesn't have a supervisor on the floor, we still join together and do what we have to," said a four-year saleswoman, "whatever is right for the employees I am with because I am an employee." A one-year specialist found that in her department, "we have our own little family. If I need someone to help me with a Macy's card or help making the goal and I do what I need for them then they will help me." A four-year specialist similarly described "a rule [in his department] that if you make your goal, leave the register and let your colleagues work, let them make their goal." And a two-year salesman found the 2011 prestrike protests engendered solidarity: "Everybody was amped, everybody was together, they were like 'let's strike!' There was a unity in there." But the seven-year salesman and shop steward highlighted the tension between union allegiance and quota competition: "I'm competing with the people I have to defend in an investigatory interview with security or HR. I'm the shop steward, but nonetheless I have to compete with them for sales. . . . It makes it more difficult."

At Target such competition was absent because there were no individual sales goals. Exposed to more collectivized incentives, Target workers exhibited greater solidarity than their Macy's counterparts.

"The best aspect of working at Target," stated a three-year salesman, "is the social atmosphere. I always make new friends there; it is not so excruciating when you got people that are friendly and cool." A first-year saleswoman asserted that before coming to work every day, "I want to see my coworkers. Today I will have mad fun because I know two of my coworkers are here." "You feel like it's friendly and open," remarked a two-year cashier, "it's not just like, 'oh I'm part of a team'—you *are* part of the team."

Target workers used words like "friend," "family," "fun," and the "one team, one dream" motto to describe their relations with each other. A first-year saleswoman and former Macy's worker described the difference between the two firms:

> It's like one team, one dream so if one person fails then everybody fails; if one person doesn't get it done, everybody doesn't get it [at Target]. They are more like a group, they want everybody to be like a family. In Macy's they were trying to individualize you; you didn't get this many cards this month and you didn't get this many sales this month.

When I asked a first-year salesman about competition with co-workers, he replied, "Nah, we don't do that." And a one-year stock-worker stated, "I am not working for myself, I am working for the team—when it is good, it is good for all, when it is bad, bad for all. I don't see it as competition, but my team leader, maybe he sees it as competition." Target's teamwork mantra had influenced his and others' views, encouraging solidarity rather than, as the Macy's salesman put it, "pitt[ing] worker against worker."

But were a collectivized process and managerial team building the only reasons for Target workers' solidarity? Closer analysis points to age and ethnicity as well. "I am twenty," said a first-year saleswoman. "There is another coworker who is twenty, one is twenty-one, my favorite coworker is twenty-three—mostly in their twenties." "Do you hang out with people outside of work?" I asked. "Yeah," she replied, "but the older ones I won't hang out with." Another first-year saleswoman in her early twenties found that "the majority of the younger people—the old people not really—hang out on their break." For those who shared a Caribbean heritage, this was another source of camaraderie. "People have a common background," said a four-year salesman and Caribbean immigrant about his Target store. "Some of my managers are American and actually you hear them speaking in the accent of the [Caribbean] people, so it influences them. If you look at everybody you can really tell who is American and who's not. So yeah, I think Caribbean people influence this store."

Age and ethnicity also excluded, particularly older workers and non-Caribbeans. A one-year saleswoman in her late twenties, although "friendly" with her coworkers, "like[d] my managers more, because they are more around my age. The coworkers is just drama, drama, drama." An eleven-year saleswoman in her sixties thought her younger coworkers "talk[ed] too much, they bring in their cell phones. . . . I feel like I'm a very hard worker," she continued, "and some people bother me, the other associates." And the seven-year saleswoman also felt age exclusion: "I want to work in peace. I'm not into all this 'he said/she said,' 'did you see what she was wearing?' No, I am too old for that."

The gap in solidarity between Macy's and Target could be traced to differences in the labor process and managerial ideology, but age and ethnicity were additional forces in the formation of workplace connections. At Target, where more were young and Caribbean than at Macy's, such shared identities augmented an already group-oriented ethos promoted by management. As the next section shows, however, solidarity was neither identical nor even strongly related to opposition, contradicting the "stageist" approaches to class consciousness of Michael Mann (1973) and Anthony Giddens (1980).

Opposition

Opposition means seeing one's interests as contrary to management's. On this score, Macy's workers were more oppositional than their Target peers, and this was reinforced by the presence of Local 1-S in its organized stores. The seven-year salesman and shop steward commented that "it's a rarity to find managers you can get along with. When that happens they tend to move that manager out." "The recognition they pretend to give at store rallies," he continued, "it's all propaganda. The associates don't buy into it—they know it's not real." Another shop steward and eight-year saleswoman described how she and her coworkers "broke down" overbearing managers:

> We had to force people to write grievances. I wrote so many grievances—if they even looked at me funny I wrote a grievance. As far as I'm concerned, that's a form of harassment. When a manager gets too many grievances they ship him out of the store.

A first-year support worker found her supervisor regularly calling on her off days: "I told her, 'don't call me on my days off.' She got the message. The union rep was like, 'if she gets annoying, just come to me.'" A two-year saleswoman at a nonunion store thought her managers "try to divide us with personal relationships, so you have to create boundaries—you have to stand your ground." And a six-year specialist described managers in explicit class terms:

> It's like a class system. I went to one staff party and observed the managers. They went by themselves: it was like a peasant class over here and

the upper class on that side; the management and the little people. I
noticed that and I didn't go back, and I encourage people not to participate in that.

Why did Macy's workers so often feel this way? Sales quotas were
a prime cause. "Their tactics when their numbers are down," stated
an eleven-year saleswoman, "is not to be desired. You shouldn't be
penalized or made to feel discouraged or threatened—that doesn't
help your outcome." The thirty-one-year salesman called it "an unfair system," a two-year saleswoman thought "they need to get rid
of it," and another two-year saleswoman felt that "no matter how
hard you work, it ain't good enough." Low pay and managers' condescending style were also reasons for opposition. "Honestly?" asked
a four-year specialist. "We are just a number, we are not a person,
it doesn't matter how hard I work. And I really hate that word 'appreciate,' 'I appreciate that'—it's a fake thing." "Their stock is doing
great," said the thirty-one-year salesman, "I wish we could take that
money." And a two-year support worker also thought "this company
is doing very well. They don't want to give you a good raise, they
don't want to give you more money, but if you walk in here on winter, summer, all of those four seasons, you will see decorations."

Younger Macy's workers were less oppositional. A salesman in
his early twenties believed "our managers are like our guide—if
we show them that we do our job then we are opening doors."
"It's pretty good," said a saleswoman in her early twenties about
relations with managers. "It's pretty casual and friendly, I don't really have complaints." A two-year salesman in his midtwenties had
more mixed experiences, seeking out "certain managers because I
know they work" and avoiding others because "they forget to put
in a personal day or forget to fill out some form." "The best manager in my department," he noted, "used to be an associate."

Among Target workers, outright opposition was rare. An electronics salesman noted, "I am pretty cool with [my manager]. I joke around with him, he jokes around with me. . . . I don't feel like there is any separation." A first-year saleswoman praised "this open-door policy. The man in charge of the whole store, we can talk to him about anything." Another first-year saleswoman compared her experience at Target with her previous job at Macy's:

> I think Target is better than Macy's because Macy's didn't recognize you for the work you do. They give you Macy's money here and there but you have to be great. At Target they have these great team member cards that we can write for each other and team leads.

When asked whether he and his managers were on the same team, a first-year salesman replied, "Yes, I feel like that; everybody's cool." A three-year food server described manager interactions as "good" because they were informal: "You come to work and someone's talking about the basketball game that happened last night—it's not like 'you can't talk to me.'" And a first-year saleswoman from the same store described her managers as "all fun, I joke around with our managers all the time. They like to raise our spirits, to make sure we're happy, to make sure we're doing what we have to do and not be angry all day. They are basically looking out for you, that's what I think."

Sentiments like these, which predominated among Target respondents, were the opposite of opposition: they displayed fellow feeling, even solidarity with management, or at least individual managers. And this was in line with Target's goals: a team-based workforce where the team included not only frontline staff but first-, second-, and third-tier supervisors. The company's open-door policy, in-store counselors, free food, huddles, and recognition helped form such bonds. The first-year saleswoman who previously worked at Macy's felt Target was better partly because "last week we did really good so they gave us Chinese food." A first-year cashier who found Target managers "very open people, nice" thought so because of the in-store counseling: "If you have any trouble, any kind of problem they can help you—if you need legal assistance there is also help that the team leaders can give you." And a one-year salesman who felt supervisors were "basically our coworkers" attributed this to participation in huddles where "we actually get a breakdown, we get a perspective of what's going to happen on that very day." When I asked if this was the case at his previous retail job, he said, "We got our sales target and everything but it's just not Target, that's all; it's just not Target. There is no other way of putting it."

Warmth and appreciation were by no means unanimous. The seven-year saleswoman found team leaders "manipulative. If you have something to say [about them], don't spread it around, go over to the [HR] office and say 'I disagree with this and this.'" As to her immediate supervisor, "I don't trust her," she said. "If I have a problem I go to my big boss, my exec." A one-year saleswoman who was "pretty cool with managers" noted that "certain ones will talk to you in a way that is not polite, like they never worked a day in their life and don't know how to talk to people." Derek, the first-year stock worker who thought his managers were rarely fun or friendly, attributed this to his department being

> behind closed doors. We say some of the filthiest things to each other, cursing and yelling. Sometimes it is joking, but when you are trying to enforce your authority on another individual, you have to choose your words carefully and the tone you use to talk to them because sometimes it doesn't work out too well [when supervisors do this].

But age differences also played a role. Across both firms, workers over thirty were much more likely to oppose management, and Target simply had far fewer in this bracket. It was thus hard to disentangle department dynamics and managerial team building from worker backgrounds in the production of shop-floor consent.

Though Macy's and Target workers were neither all negative nor all positive about their managers, clear patterns of opposition at the first and collaboration at the second prevailed. Opposition at Macy's was often directed at the quota system, low wages, and managers' condescension and was more common among older, long-term workers. Target managers' participatory overtures, combined with union absence and a younger, short-term workforce contributed to vertical solidarity in its stores. This disparity paralleled that in union support.

On Unions

How did retail workers feel about unions? At Macy's this was not abstract: Local 1-S had organized several of its stores longer than anyone could remember and a complex contractual relationship with management had evolved. The question before them was whether their experience with Local 1-S was positive or negative. At Target and at nonunion Macy's, unions were abstract, and questions about them pertained not to any particular organization but to the idea of worker representation, which was often unfamiliar. Much like opposition and job identity, union support was more widespread at Macy's—union and nonunion—than at Target. But some unionized workers had criticisms, just as several Target workers wanted to be organized.

Most Macy's workers liked Local 1-S. "With the union there is job security," said a two-year support worker, "They can't fire you

unless you are doing something unethical. . . . I like the union."
When asked if he would participate in a hypothetical strike, he replied without hesitation, "Yeah, I would take part in it." A one-year
saleswoman found that "the union does hold a lot of power. If you
have any little issue you can always go to the union, they are always
there to help." "I've never been in a union before," said a two-year
saleswoman, "but I'm glad we have a union because the workers
here have protection. . . . Some think the union is worthless, but
from what I've seen they're doing their job." For a first-year salesman, "this is my first union experience" and it was "pretty cool. It's
nice to have somebody have your back." A two-year saleswoman
who had "never been in a unionized system before," felt that "after
the [almost] strike, the psychology changed between manager and
worker. I felt that we were untouchable. I could tell managers kind
of backed off. They were no longer as abrasive; there was a definite
line drawn." "It makes sense," said a one-year salesman about the
union, "because it really gets your back."

But others criticized Local 1-S. The six-year specialist who described sales staff as "peasants" and managers as "upper class" had
similar disdain for the union:

> Union experience? Useless, helpless, I don't know. Macy's has more per-
> suasive power than the union. The only time they [the union] will step
> in is when there are people they are trying to fire; otherwise they are just
> collecting [dues]. And whatever policy the union favors tends to work
> better with the older people.

A first-year specialist felt the new contract gave raises "only [to]
employees who have been here a certain number of years," and a
four-year specialist who thought the union should have struck in
2011 didn't "care about the union because if the company doesn't
want me the union can't do nothing." "This layer," he said about

long-term members, "for them it is good, but not for us. With the new contract, new hires will not get any benefits, and they agreed with that. That's why I'm done with this union."

Those who opposed unions in general often cited their work ethic and ability for why they "didn't need" one; some saw Local 1-S's acceptance of low wages and benefits as evidence of this. Yet a few prounion workers voiced similar critiques. Ethel, the eight-year saleswoman and shop steward encountered earlier, thought "we should've had a strike," and the seven-year salesman and shop steward said, with regard to the quota system, "I don't think the union has put up enough resistance. We have put up resistance in shop steward meetings but I think the union has to allow Macy's to run their business. I always say the union is not perfect, but the company is not perfect." These views recall the "rebel rank-and-file" of 1970s America—workers who were organized and prounion but felt sold out by their leaders and often led wildcat strikes (Brenner, Brenner, and Winslow. 2010; Cowie 2010).

At nonunion Macy's, support for unions was thinner. A first-year saleswoman shared the views of others in being "glad we don't do unions." Her opinion was heavily influenced by management propaganda. "At the meetings," she stated, "they tell you, 'if you want to be in a union, you are always free to do so, but once people start joining unions, they gonna try to take over the entire store.'" A first-year saleswoman said she didn't want a union because her previous experience with one was bad: "The union I was in, I really didn't like it. They were taking money out of my check and they didn't help me with anything."

But some nonunion Macy's workers also wanted to be organized. "I know a lot about unions," said a second-year saleswoman.

Since I come here [to the United States] in 1999 I worked in a union job. I was in Local 1199 [health care workers]. This here is my only job without a union, so I know about unions. They fight for my rights, we fight, we won. It works for you, you've got somebody talking for you, you've got somebody voting for you. So I think we need a union.

"I love unions, are you kidding me?" asked a first-year merchandiser. "My mom was a social worker and she was a big supporter of AFSCME [American Federation of State, County, and Municipal Employees]." And a two-year salesman believed

> a union would give the employees more of a voice and more oomph into what happens. It probably wouldn't change too much because it's still Macy's policy. But the way it seems, my father's union is good because he does construction, so if he finishes a temporary job, they find him another one immediately.

Union support was thus far from absent among nonunion Macy's workers and often stemmed from personal or family experience. Active antiunionists were sometimes influenced by negative past experience but more often by dubious claims from management.

Target workers were less supportive. While some were adamantly antiunion, most were simply unfamiliar with the concept. A two-year cashier, when asked if she was familiar with unions, replied simply, "No, I don't know how that works." Neither did a first-year cashier: "I don't know how the union works; I don't have any idea about the union so I don't know how they could help me." A first-year saleswoman mistakenly believed "they [Target workers] have one but most people aren't in it." And a one-year salesman, when asked what he thought about unions replied, "I don't care about it, I don't know about it, I don't involve myself with it. If they give me a little more information about it I will talk about it but it's never really been brought up to me, so it's not my business."

Most Target workers simply didn't know what unions were and consequently couldn't support them. Others, however, were actively antiunion. A one-year saleswoman who strongly opposed management also strongly opposed unions: "Joyce Leslie [her previous employer] was a union store and that was the worst! The break room was bad, the refrigerator didn't work half the time. It was really bad, I didn't like it." I asked if she thought a union could address her issues at Target: "Nope," she replied. An eleven-year saleswoman thought "No, we don't need [a union] here, everybody would go out on strike. We have a health insurance, we have dental and all that," though she, like most others, was not enrolled in either. A two-year salesman had "a family member that is a union member, but I myself don't have a particular interest in unions. I'm a person that would rather manage." And the first-year saleswoman who once worked at a unionized Macy's didn't "think there is really a difference, I don't really think [a union] would make things better. Target already has this balance."

As at nonunion Macy's, Target's nonsupporters often derived their opinions from management's disinformation. A first-year stock worker noted that a few months before our interview, "they [managers] would speak to us individually, pick out certain people and talk to us about joining the union. [They would say] 'if you want to join the union, by all means, go ahead.' But after the discussion most of us were like 'no' for the union." I asked whether this was his current view. "Yes," he replied, "no one wants to join the union really." A one-year stock worker similarly announced, "If they [union representatives] come by I'm not signing it because I don't want to be part of it." I asked him why, and he answered,

Because of what they [managers] said, that the union doesn't keep promises. Oh you will get more hours, more vacation time and stuff like that, they will tell you things like that but when you contact them they won't pick up the phone, so it's not a good idea.

Yet despite Target's systematic union bashing, several wanted to be organized. "How do you feel about unions?" I asked a four-year salesman, who answered,

> I think there should be [one] because some of the things that have happened, it's unfair. If there was a union we would be getting paid more. They should assign somebody to do garbage—sometimes they assign us and we don't have gloves or anything and we risk being infected. There are areas where there should be a union to help us out.

According to a first-year saleswoman, if there were a union at her store, "it would be more fair. Some things are not fair, like we usually don't get the shifts that we want." The seven-year saleswoman had "been in jobs with unions and the reason they [Target managers] don't want a union is because that cutting hours, that favoritism, will stop. That's why they don't want a union. I am in favor of the union, but nobody else is." The active support of several other colleagues indicated she was partly mistaken in this final claim.

Comparing workers' union attitudes is different from comparing their identity, solidarity, or opposition. At some Macy's stores, unionism was concrete: it was part of workers' daily experience, and their opinions reflected this. At nonunion stores, unionism was more abstract but still influenced by the companies' specific antiunion propaganda and some individuals' past experience. Overall, most who were currently unionized liked it: organized workers were consistently more prounion than their unorganized peers, while antiunionism among this latter group often resulted from a combination of unfamiliarity and management dissuasion. Moreover, union support paralleled feelings of job identity and opposition but not those of solidarity. How did these views relate to those on U.S. society more generally?

Beyond the Sales Floor

> America is supposed to be all capitalist but it really is a monopoly. It is really hard to get to the top. They will sell you the American dream with the house and the picket fence and the dog, and you will think you're going to do it, but it is so not true. You just have to find your niche, hopefully it pays and be happy with it. (First-year Macy's saleswoman)

Class consciousness extends beyond the workplace. It involves the totality of social relationships and alternative ways of organizing them. Labor historians have often perceived a disjunction between what Selig Perlman calls "job consciousness" (1928, 169) and class consciousness, between what Ira Katznelson (1982, 6) describes as "the radical separation . . . of the politics of work from the politics of community" and what Howard Kimmeldorf (1999, 4) identifies as an "unusual combination of political quiescence and industrial revolt" among American workers (see also Halle 1984). Those at Macy's and Target, as we've seen, displayed a mixed bag of identity, opposition, pro- and antiunionism, and these largely tracked each firm's labor regime and individuals' life positions. But did these workers also display conservatism in line with the classic American paradigm? The answer, in short, is no.

Most of those I interviewed were dissatisfied with "the system" as they saw it, regardless of whether they worked for Macy's or Target or at union or nonunion stores. "You can't even get public housing, you can't even get public grants no more," said a four-year Macy's saleswoman. "If you had to use the system," she explained, referring to her youth, "it was useful; now when you go in there the system is messed up. The system is not the way it once was—our generation now, it's not the way we grew up. We had people locked up and incarcerated then but now it's more." A ten-year Macy's saleswoman also used "system" to refer to public assistance but interpreted it as too generous rather than too stingy:

> Unemployment is so high, some of the people are depending on the system, as we call it lazy. So it is sucking, it is pulling the entire economy down. Whereas we have to get up in the morning and go out and make a living. It's so hard for us. It puts us in a situation where, maybe we should just go on the system too?

A one-year Target stock worker and recent immigrant spoke of the system in describing the American economy and workplace:

> People say back in Africa that America is heaven. But to me, everything depends on the individual. I have not been disappointed. I think the American system is very smart as compared to Ghana. Here, everything moves with a sense of urgency. The system is fast.

And a first-year Macy's saleswoman responded to my question about U.S. society and politics with the same term:

> I don't know much about the general political system, but it's a tough economy. Companies are trying to cut costs any way they can, either merchandise or labor. I don't see me working anytime soon for fourteen or fifteen dollars an hour, unless I've been here twenty years.

"System" and words like "economy," "city," "government," and "country" were used to indicate forces beyond respondents' control. Whether viewing these positively, as did the young man from Ghana, or negatively, as did most others, most framed such issues in fatalistic language. "The low wages at Macy's are NAFTA's fault," said a first-year visual merchandiser. "They created this 'free trade' area where people are getting paid crap and have no rights." A seven-year Target saleswoman said she didn't vote anymore "because none of them are good. They promise you, promise you, promise you until they get into office. Then the things I see disgust me." A first-year Macy's saleswoman didn't "get into politics. I am so against government. But not only government [in general], it is our government." A first-year Target saleswoman held similar views:

> I feel like there is a lot of hidden money in the [United] States. . . . I definitely think politicians and government can do more to create jobs for us. I just think they are being greedy with the money or they are holding onto it for some odd reason.

And an eight-year Macy's saleswoman used the language of Occupy Wall Street:

> I understand the 99 percent. I believe that corporations—first I should say the Republicans—are trying to get rid of all unions. They are for corporations; I mean they bail out the banks but they garnish my wages. When I went to college I took out a credit card, which I would never do again.

The ubiquity of opinions like these, which cast deep suspicion and even disgust on government and corporations, exposed greater alienation from U.S. institutions than from Macy's or Target as particular employers. Some couched their critiques in class terms. "People become rich and famous off things like online news channels, whereas those of us who've been working for forty years never really make it" said a first-year Macy's saleswoman. A two-year saleswoman believed politicians' agenda was "not that of the 99 percent! It's obviously the wealthy and business who hire these wealthy people to go to Washington." Mann (1973) might have called these views "class totality": seeing class divisions as the defining feature of society. And one respondent, a four-year Macy's saleswoman, articulated what Mann might have deemed "a conception of an *alternative* society"—or at least of firm ownership:

> *A:* Everybody [management] is doing what they want to do, because it's not run by the city, the city don't have nothing to do with it.
>
> *Q:* You think Macy's would be different if it was publicly owned?
>
> *A:* City-owned? Yeah, I think it would. I think it would be more secure if it was city-owned. When it's personal they can flip things around and there's nothing you can do about it because it's not city-owned. . . . I would rather that the city owned it because you would be more protected just like regular city jobs.

Not as radical but equally positive were the proposals of a first-year Macy's visual merchandiser:

> *Q:* Do you think there could be any political solution to the problem of low pay?
>
> *A:* Yeah, like raising the minimum wage. I think the union would be the ultimate solution, but community organizing—I spent years doing it and don't feel much hope for their success. It would have to be something all-encompassing with the laws, raising minimum wage, getting rid of some of the free trade laws that make it possible for the company make money selling five-dollar T-shirts.

Systemic proposals for change, however, were rare. Most saw the political system and economy as indifferent to their interests and instead reached for individual solutions. Education was prominent. "A lot of people want to move up," said a three-year Target food server, and they do, because a lot of people are in school, and that's all you really need for this place is a degree. Most places, if you get that college degree then you move right on up. At Target, with the degree, they will put you right in, "where do you need to be?"

A first-year Target cashier who thought it "almost impossible" to support herself on Target wages and lived with her mother at the time said her goal was to become a schoolteacher. "I really hope so. I was thinking of a backup plan if that doesn't work out and I go to school for years to get my degree." And a two-year Macy's saleswoman felt "the most important thing is to have an education. The government has passed all of these laws because a lot of people aren't educated. If people paid more attention, if they were educated enough, certain things wouldn't happen."

College credentials, however, were seen by some not as a pathway to success but as a barrier to escape from low-wage work. "I guess it's decent," said a three-year Target salesman, "for the job that it is. It's retail: you don't have to have a degree, you could just get a GED, you could have even been locked up, there is really no major credential to work here, all you need is a high school diploma and you're hired." "The guy in charge of that whole Target," stated a first-year saleswoman at the same store, "him and his wife work in Target and they both have high positions. But to get those positions, you have to have an education."

Q: You mean like a bachelor's degree?

A: Yeah, they push you to go to school so that you could get to those positions eventually.

Q: Do you think you need a bachelor's to do that job?

A: I think you could do it just by having been there for a while. I don't think it's nothing too crazy.

In general, most were dissatisfied with the state of the economy and distrustful of politicians and corporations (though not always those they worked for), and many framed these issues in class-like terms. The only exceptions were three young men—recent immigrants well on their way toward a bachelor's degree. One of them, a Target cashier, thought

> life in my country and here is much different. [Bangladesh] is a Third World country; living there is really hard and all the politics is really bad. Here the security is good, the job is good. Getting a job in my country is really, really hard. You have to give someone from the company a bribe.

Such optimism, based on comparison of the United States with his country of origin, was lacking among most of his peers.

Although most did not seek systemic alternatives, where a nascent movement was present (Occupy Wall Street), several used its slogans to articulate grievances. This hints at the potential for new social movements, such as the Fight for 15 or Black Lives Matter, both of which have emerged since these interviews were conducted, to reframe individual problems as social issues that can be collectively challenged.

Contrasted with their workplace views, the political disillusionment of these retail workers marked a reversal of the historic pattern of "industrial militancy and political quiescence." While displaying a mix of opposition and consent in the workplace, their political attitudes were anything but quiescent. It is hard to say whether this resulted from living in New York—America's most unequal city (Monaghan and Ikeler 2014) with a vibrant left and labor history (Freeman 2000)—or from many respondents' black identities and experience of marginalization in U.S. society. Whatever the cause, such discontent could facilitate organizing if the connections between political and workplace oppression could be drawn and positive change—such as the $15 minimum wage—made tangible.

The Role of the Service Labor Process

At face value, the differences between Macy's and Target workers support the idea that workplace experience shapes consciousness. But face values can deceive. Here I dig beneath the surface by comparing workplace and demographic differences to assess the real sources of workers' views. To make this possible, I carefully reviewed interview transcripts for the seventy-two directly employed and nonsupervisory respondents and coded each as having job identity or not, solidarity with coworkers or not, opposition to management or not, and being prounion or not. I then looked to see whether these binary constructions varied meaningfully between firms and workplaces as well as among the various nonclass groups labor scholars see as important.

The results of these comparisons are presented in table 6.1. Majority views for a given group are shaded in gray, and a summated scale of all four dimensions included, with means above 2 also shaded. These figures should be read with caution because the samples on which they are based were small and not systematically selected; it is thus unclear how much these workers' views represent those within their respective workplaces or demographic groups. Nevertheless, suggestive patterns emerge that challenge received wisdom about class consciousness and its sources.

First, the workplace. Though I interviewed fewer nonunion than unionized Macy's workers, the views of each group differed only slightly, and the overall spread was largely the same as of the

TABLE 6.1

Class consciousness by workplace and demographic characteristics

		Job identity	Solidarity	Opposition	Prounion	0–4 Scale (mean)
Workplace						
Macy's (N = 41)	Unionized (N = 29)	17 (59%)	13 (45%)	19 (66%)	17 (59%)	2.28
	Nonunion (N = 12)	7 (58%)	3 (25%)	7 (58%)	6 (50%)	1.92
	Total	24 (59%)	16 (39%)	26 (63%)	23 (56%)	2.17
Target (N = 31)		5 (16%)	22 (71%)	11 (35%)	11 (35%)	1.58
Age						
30 and older (N = 24)		18 (75%)	9 (38%)	18 (75%)	18 (75%)	2.63
Under 30 (N = 48)		11 (23%)	29 (60%)	19 (40%)	16 (33%)	1.56
Gender						
Female (N = 43)		20 (47%)	17 (40%)	25 (58%)	21 (49%)	1.93
Male (N = 29)		9 (31%	21 (72%)	12 (41%)	13 (45%)	1.90
Race						
Black (N = 49)		17 (35%)	26 (53%)	26 (53%)	22 (45%)	1.86
Non-black (N = 23)		12 (52%)	12 (52%)	11 (48%)	12 (52%)	2.04
Nativity						
Foreign-born (N = 23)		7 (30%)	10 (43%)	11 (48%)	10 (43%)	1.65
U.S.-born (N = 49)		22 (45%)	28 (57%)	26 (53%)	24 (29%)	2.04

unionized sample alone. On all except solidarity, Macy's workers were more consistently class-conscious than their Target counterparts. In their own explanations, identity seemed to flow from Macy's workers' more complex and engaging work, their lack of solidarity from the competitive design of sales, their opposition from adversarial managers, and their prounion attitudes from the same source as well as from positive experience with Local 1-S.

Target workers' solidarity, in turn, seemed to flow from team-based collectivism in their workplaces, but on all other counts they were less class conscious than Macy's workers.

Age, however, was also important. Table 6.1 shows that respondents over thirty were consistently more oppositional, more job conscious, and more prounion, though they had less solidarity than their under-thirty counterparts, contributing to their greater overall class consciousness. This marked difference seemed to come from older workers' lack of alternatives, their greater dependence on wages, and greater commitment to their current jobs—most were not just passing through retail on their way to a degree or a higher-paid job. Younger workers, for their part, showed more fellow feeling, mainly for each other (the majority at both firms) but also for their older colleagues. Though it complicates matters that 40 percent of Macy's but only 23 percent of Target respondents were over thirty, the analysis in chapter 5 identified workers' age—particularly their youth—as a defining feature of contingent control, fully developed at Target. It is thus not merely happenstance that Target workers tended to be younger than their Macy's peers and that these same workers tended to be less class-conscious; rather, their attitudes, flexibility, and expectations were deliberately sought.

Gender is an axis of job segregation that many also see influencing workplace views (Hartmann 1981; Jones 2001). Here, however, it made little difference. Though female respondents had more job identity, less solidarity, and more opposition than males, these differences were small, while their union support and overall class consciousness were nearly identical to men's. Thus despite sex-typing at Macy's and Target—the placing of salespersons in like-gendered departments and women more often in interactive roles that paid less—women were not much more class-conscious than men. More Macy's respondents were female than Target respondents (64 versus 52 percent), and the similar patterns in solidarity and opposition between male/female and Macy's/Target workers may also reflect this.

Race presented a more complicated picture. The majority of those I interviewed identified as black, including those of African American, Afro-Caribbean, and West African backgrounds. Compared with the eleven white, six Asian, and six Latino respondents, black workers were less job conscious, more opposed to management, less prounion, and generally more class-conscious than their non-black peers. As with gender, however, these differences were not very big (with the possible exception of job identity), and though race has often been a major contributor to solidarity, this was not the case here: black and non-black workers showed the same degree of solidarity with coworkers. Furthermore, black workers made up roughly equal shares of Macy's (64 percent) and Target (71 percent) respondents, so differences between them and their non-black colleagues explain little variation between firms.

Last was nativity. Immigrants have been central to recent attempts to revive the U.S. labor movement, with Milkman (2006) and Ness (2005) arguing that they are often more class-conscious and ready to organize than their native-born peers—largely because they suffer more systematic workplace oppression. Here, however, although immigrant workers were more prounion than the native-born, on all other measures they were less class-conscious. Immigrant status thus broadly mitigated, rather than accelerated, class consciousness among these workers. And again, since the foreign-born made up similar shares of Macy's and Target respondents (34 and 32 percent, respectively), their views cannot explain much of the difference between firms.

So which is it that explains workers' views? The labor process, employment relations, or workers' demographics? The standard way of answering such questions is through multivariate analysis, which these data are neither large nor systematic enough to support. But workers' own explanations point to a significant influence of work experience: whether managers were harsh or friendly, whether tasks were engaging or rote, competitive or cooperative, and whether wages and benefits met their expectations. This last point also explains the importance of age, which largely overlapped with workers' financial needs. Target, with its regime of contingent control, deliberately hired younger, more transient workers than Macy's, as seen in chapter 5. Age and workplace, at least in department store retail, were thus not independent but codependent. Gender, race, and nativity, though affecting how some workers felt about their jobs, were indeed more external than internal to the low-wage sales process.

THIS CHAPTER EXAMINED workers' class consciousness across five broad dimensions. It found clear differences on the first four (identity, solidarity, opposition and unionism) based on workers' employer, their age, and to some extent their gender, race, and nativity. But politically they were almost universally dissatisfied with the status quo and deeply distrusted politicians. Two lessons stand out from this. The first is that class consciousness does not always proceed in linear fashion—it does not move predictably from identity to solidarity to opposition, as the models of Mann (1973) and Giddens (1980) suggest. Instead, as Macy's workers show, it may jump or skip levels, and workplace solidarity is not always a necessary part. Job identity, however, does appear strongly related to opposition and union support; it may thus provide an inroad to organizing that few besides

Dorothy Sue Cobble (1991b) have considered. The second lesson is that some service workers—particularly those in large, unequal cities and from marginalized ethnic or racial groups—have deep political grievances that go against the historical pattern among American workers (Katznelson 1982; Kimmeldorf 1999). These grievances, as the next chapter makes clear, may provide further inroads to organizing.

7

Service Worker Organizing

A few months after the bulk of the interviews for this book were completed, a movement of retail and fast-food workers burst onto the scene. On the day after Thanksgiving ("Black Friday"), 2012, hundreds of protests were held in Walmart parking lots and storefronts around the country against the firm's egregious labor practices. These walkouts and rallies were coordinated by a new nonunion organization—OUR Walmart—which, although initiated by the UFCW, involved frontline workers in planning and execution. Every year since, Black Friday protests have been repeated and grown, drawing increased media attention and raising the issue of worker exploitation at the nation's largest retailer. These annual actions have been complemented in the interim by minority strikes at key Walmart stores and by principled acts of civil disobedience (Miles 2013). Though they have not yet achieved collective bargaining or major changes in the company's employment regime, these symbolic protests have penetrated public consciousness and pushed Walmart to improve its pregnant-worker policies and raise its wage floor first to $9 and then to $10 an hour.

About a week after the first Black Friday protest, several hundred fast-food workers walked off their jobs and rallied for "$15 and a union" in New York City. This was more surprising than the actions at Walmart since the SEIU, which organized the struggle, kept its plans more secret. Since that rally, a series of others have been held in cities across the country, growing larger and larger each time. This national movement and its local formations— Fight for 15, Fast Food Forward, and others—have pushed city governments in Chicago and Kansas City to raise their minimum wage to $13; Seattle, San Francisco, and Los Angeles to $15; and New York State to raise the minimum wage in the fast-food industry also to $15. As Patrick McGeehan of the *New York Times* put it, "The labor protest movement that fast-food workers in New York City began nearly three years ago has led to higher wages for workers all across the country. On Wednesday, it paid off for the people who started it" (July 22, 2015).

The movement of low-wage service workers has begun to taste success. It is showing that "bad" service jobs are not an unalterable fact of life but a social construct that can be challenged. What then can the workplace-level insights of this book teach that we don't already know? As labor journalist Steven Greenhouse (2015) pointed out, $15 and a union "are two very different things." OUR Walmart and the Fight for 15 have pushed some local politicians to raise minimum wages by utilizing what Jennifer Chun (2009) calls "symbolic leverage": appealing to social morality through small-scale but visible actions that shame corporations and draw attention to workers' plight. Such "naming and shaming" can transform public opinion and goad politicians into action. It can also pressure consumer-oriented companies into allowing—or at least not fighting—unionization, as SEIU's Justice for Janitors and the California farm workers' struggle showed (Milkman 2006; Ganz 2009). But symbolic leverage ultimately depends on the cooperation of elites to be effective. It is government officials who enact minimum-wage laws, corporate executives who sign neutrality agreements, and large foundations that increasingly fund many nonunion workers' groups, OUR Walmart included (Fine 2005). Symbolic actions can aid in this process of achieving what Jenkins (2002) calls "advocacy" rather than "organizing" or what Milkman (2006) calls "top-down" rather than "bottom-up" change. Only large groups of workers, however, can organize a union and make it effective.

This book has interrogated the sources of such bottom-up power in the retail workplace. It has looked at the organization and relations of selling to see whether they produce a consciousness that could enable what Wright (2000) calls "associational power." In chapter 2 I took a historical overview of U.S. retail, showing that its long-term development was not much different from classic patterns in manufacturing, whereby small, labor-intensive firms combined into fewer and larger corporations that dominated markets and used increasingly capital-intensive processes. American retail unions followed the arc of their industrial counterparts, growing rapidly in the 1930s and '40s, reaching their peak in the postwar era, and then quickly unraveling after 1980. But their arc was smaller: retail unions never represented even a fifth of retail workers and were overwhelmingly concentrated in supermarkets and urban department stores. The remnants of the latter still exist today at firms like Macy's, but their isolation has forced them to accept deep concessions on wages and benefits. Entire subsectors and regions were never organized, allowing for the proliferation of paternalist, antiunion regimes like Target's.

The comparison of Macy's and Target showed that service work can be highly collectivized. At Target this went along with lower control and task complexity for workers. Though Macy's displayed similar tendencies, its process was specialized by department, brand, and price, and its salespersons maintained a semiskilled, individualized approach. It was therefore an eroded craft system. Target's process no longer involved individual persuasion of customers by knowledgeable sales staff; it instead involved self-service shopping aided by store design, just-in-time replenishment, friendly assistance, and centralized checkout. Target's system, with frequent rotation, teamwork, and flexible scheduling, bore many similarities to that of Japanese automakers, earning it the name service Toyotism.

When I examined employment relations, I found that the eroded craft model went hand in hand with adversarialism and service Toyotism with low-cost paternalism. Both Macy's and Target were "low-road" employers that provided minimal wages and benefits, yet while Macy's managers encouraged competition and were often unapproachable, those at Target were up close and personal, monitoring and directing workers with a softer, informal style. Target also provided more perks like free food, counseling, and recognition that engendered a team-oriented ethos. Much of this was linked to concerted union avoidance also present at non-union Macy's but notably absent from its unionized stores. Adversarialism and paternalism, however, were used by both companies to manage older and younger workers, respectively. Macy's simply hired more middle-aged workers than Target, whose workforce was mostly under thirty and often in college. Age and life position were thus intertwined with occupation and the style of supervision workers encountered.

Chapter 5 looked at how these forces combined in the ongoing transformation of services. I compared Macy's and Target's as older and newer sales models and argued that de-skilling, defined as declining complexity and autonomy of tasks, was the clearest trajectory for retail salespersons. Their degradation parallels past transformations in manufacturing, where skilled craft workers were replaced by semiskilled operatives, but in services this has happened on an emotional rather than a physical plane. Salespersons who once engaged in personalized deep acting are increasingly performing generic surface acting, if any, beyond their stocking and maintenance duties. The conception aspects of selling—knowledge and persuasion—are increasingly separated from their execution on the sales floor. The end point of these changes would be complete automation, already evidenced at Internet retailers such as Amazon. And these shifts were found alongside those from adversarialism to paternalism and the proportional growth of a secondary workforce. Taken together, they represent an emergent regime of contingent control fully developed at Target but only partially at Macy's. Contingent control extends Edwards's (1979) schema of workplace control to capture new forms of exploitation at large service firms. It consists of contingent employment, standardized work, a benevolent bureaucracy (bad jobs but good managers), and a pliant, mostly secondary workforce.

The effects of this regime on workers' consciousness appeared to be lower job identity, opposition, and union support but higher solidarity. Macy's workers had more of the first three and Target's more of the fourth. But workplace differences evaporated when I turned to their sociopolitical views. The vast majority of those I spoke to were deeply dissatisfied with U.S. politics and the structure of U.S. society in the twenty-first century. This finding and the previously undertheorized connection between job identity and opposition have important implications for organizing, which I return to later.

Though my study largely supported received wisdom about how work shapes consciousness, surprises emerged about services. Emotional labor, which was more extensive and varied at Macy's, did not lead to a dilution of workers' job identity and opposition, a pattern suggested by others (Wharton 1993; Erickson and Wharton 1997). This challenges the idea, pervasive since Bell (1973), that services are outside the class dynamic of capitalism and unproductive of its characteristic forms of consciousness. Leidner's (1993, 1996) proposal that the "service triangle" mutes opposition was less clearly challenged. Though Macy's process encouraged stronger worker-customer and Target's stronger worker-manager alliances, these differences were not very big. Target workers' lower opposition may have come from their seeking stability in management protocol but may also have come from softer supervision, collectivized incentives, and workers' youthful optimism.

Gender, long a source of selection into service work, also divided Macy's and Target. Both firms more often placed women in interactive roles and men in noninteractive ones; among sales jobs, men were more common in high-value departments. Each dynamic created a male pay premium. But an important countertendency was the "de-gendering" of many service tasks, complemented by Target's de-gendering of product labels. Neither Macy's nor Target promoted different interactive scripts for male and female workers, with Macy's MAGIC and Target's "Fast, Fun, and Friendly" and "Can I help you find something?" being decidedly gender neutral. Perhaps because of this, men and women had few differences in consciousness.

These insights from department store retail provide basic answers to the questions that started this book. To the question *Why are unions so absent in services?* we can respond that limited structural power but also unions' strategic missteps and employers' vehement opposition are to blame. To the question *Does service work discourage class consciousness?* we can answer, not always. Even in nonunion settings I encountered many service workers who derived feelings of opposition, solidarity, and union support from their job experience, and the overall dearth of organized resistance in retail was shown to be as much historically produced as structurally determined. To the question *How is service work changing?* we can say that important sectors of it are moving from a specialized, semiskilled, adversarial model to a collectivized, de-skilled, paternalist one, both of which, however, provide low-road wages and benefits. And to the question *How do these changes shape consciousness?* we can respond that the emerging regime of contingent control reduces workers' job identity and opposition while bolstering their solidarity.

What are the lessons for service worker organizing? First, the challenges. With limited power to stop profit flow, service workers might turn to what Wright (2000) calls "marketplace structural power": limiting access to the labor market—as craft unions do—by upgrading or certifying their skills. In New York, the Retail Action Project has explored this option on a small scale with some success (Ikeler 2014). But a central finding of this book is the de-skilling of frontline sales work. What little labor market power salespersons now possess is quickly being eroded. At present, few mass retailers require much experience or training of new hires, and in a glutted low-skill job market, their freedom to discriminate in hiring or replace troublesome employees is formidable. De-skilling also creates subjective barriers to occupational identity, which, as Cobble (1991b) notes, has often been a key ingredient to organizing. At Target, which is more indicative of retail trends, only a small minority of salespersons had any job identity, and this was unsurprising since their roles had been stripped of creative, autonomous content. Combined with contingency, de-skilling thus erodes not only workers' leverage in the market but also their subjective basis for group belonging.

Managerial hegemony is another obstacle. Target's supportive supervision and teamwork ethos—combined with concerted union prevention—deeply influenced the consciousness of workers, particularly the young and inexperienced. Similar efforts were also used at nonunion and even unionized Macy's, though with limited success at the latter. As elaborated by Gramsci (1971), cultural hegemony is the domination of subaltern groups by noncoercive, ideological means. In the microcosm of the workplace, an analogous project was embodied in managers' efforts to elicit consent and vertical solidarity. These practices, however, simply paint inequality as inevitable and desirable; they do not make it so. Chapter 5 identified cracks in the hegemony of contingent control that successful organizing would need to accentuate while building upon the coworker solidarity engendered by that regime.

A final obstacle is the muted character of existing service unionism, such as at Macy's. If workers have negative experiences or perceive unions as not making much difference, this blunts the appeal of organizing. RWDSU and the broader UFCW and the separate SEIU are large organizations that employ hundreds of full-time staff, some of whom earn six-figure salaries. Yet these same organizations include dues-paying members who earn poverty wages, sometimes as little as $7.50 an hour. Leaders will undoubtedly argue that their organizations struggle in a hostile environment. And this is true. But if resources exist that could go toward organizing or more aggressive bargaining and are instead funding the salaries of top officials, this raises important questions.

Besides these obstacles there are also significant inroads to organizing. The most obvious are the conditions many service workers face: subliving wages, unaffordable benefits, and job insecurity, as well as hours and scheduling insecurity. At Target and nonunion Macy's these were all part of workers' daily lives, which at Target contrasted starkly with managers' supportive interactions. These first three issues have long motivated successful organizing in garment and auto manufacturing, in nonprofit health care and among seasonal farm laborers. Scheduling insecurity, however, is a new mode of exploitation and a new grievance that worker organizations could place front and center, as some already have (Greenhouse 2014).

Beneath employment relations the collectivization of sales work, combined with similar demographics in some sectors, is creating the basis for heightened solidarity. Group cohesion is vital to organizing, especially in the early phases when managers may intimidate or co-opt individual workers into avoiding protest, reporting their peers or voting no in certification elections. While solidarity can be built in the course of struggle even among previously indifferent workers (Fantasia 1988), its preexistence in workplaces like Target is an added advantage. The task of organizers will be to identify the sources of such solidarity—whether it is based on cooperation at work or on common identities (youth, ethnicity, etc.) outside it—and sever its extension to management.

A final inroad exists in workers' political betrayal. Although American unions have a long history of supporting Democrats (Davis 1986; Moody 2007), there is now generalized dissatisfaction with both parties, which has rarely been tapped. Campaigns to organize individual workplaces, firms, or even whole sectors could be linked to criticism of politics as usual, the influence of big business and, where possible, the role of direct employers. Some of this is already happening in the struggle for higher minimum wages, particularly in Seattle, where fast-food organizing found a voice in the insurgent city councilor Kshama Sawant. Elsewhere fast-food organizers have also exposed the vigorous lobbying of restaurant groups to keep wages down. But a more robust form might look something like the abstentionism of the Industrial Workers of the World (IWW) (in favor of direct action) or the third party challenges of early twentieth-century socialists. Both movements combined workplace agitation with a broad-based critique of American politics as corrupt and out of touch. Most of those I interviewed had similar impressions. They were likely indicative of a wider swath of U.S. workers, whom polls show are increasingly fed up with two-party politics and market fundamentalism. The mobilization of such sentiment by unions seeking to organize low-wage service workers could take the struggle well beyond symbolism and elite advocacy. Yet it is precisely beyond those stages that these movements must advance to establish their own self-sustaining power. I hope the lessons of this book will serve that end.

A Note on Class Consciousness

Class consciousness is among the most significant and controversial ideas in all of social science. This book has employed a relatively constrained version of it derived from a particular, if influential, interpretation—that of Michael Mann (1973). Here I reflect on the concept and its alternative interpretations to better situate my investigation of it. The main theoretical controversies pertain to three basic questions: (1) Who can have class consciousness? (2) What is it? and (3) How does it develop? Georg Lukács broke the first question down even further, asking whether the "the problem of class consciousness [is] a 'general' sociological problem" or whether "it mean[s] one thing for the proletariat and another for every other class" ([1923] 1971, 46). This book, along with most social research since the early twentieth century, has meant *working-class* (rather than bourgeois, petit-bourgeois, peasant or landlord) consciousness when discussing the concept, so that is my focus here.

To the question of what constitutes the working class today, there is no straightforward answer. One historically resonant definition would be all those employed in manufacturing, construction, and transportation, as well as their dependents. Such a conception is used by Andrew Cherlin (2014, 8) to depict long-run changes in the family lives of working-class men and fits well with Halle's (1984) portrait of "America's working man" as well as Marx and Engels' early description of "the proletariat" as "a class of labourers . . . enslaved by the machine . . . and, above all, by the industrial bourgeois manufacturer" ([1848] 1988, 61–62). Nicos Poulantzas (1975) carried this interpretation deep into the twentieth century, asserting that nearly all those employed outside physical goods production were part of a "new petit-bourgeoisie" and not the working class. This view is in a distinct minority today and was even undermined by Marx in volume 3 of *Capital*. There he argued with respect to "commercial" capitalists (retailers and wholesalers) that

> his profit depends on the amount of capital that he can employ in this process, and he can employ all the more capital in buying and selling, the greater the unpaid labour of his *clerks*. . . . Their unpaid labour, even though it does not create surplus-value, does create his ability to appropriate surplus-value [from industrial capital]. ([1893] 1981, 407, emphasis added)

And in volume 1 Marx proposed that "the extraordinary increase in the productivity of large-scale industry . . . permits a larger and larger part of *the working class* to be employed unproductively," i.e., outside material goods production ([1867] 1976, 574, emphasis added). Most class theorists, though they disagree about the boundaries between the working class and whatever lies above it— for example, a "professional-managerial class" (Ehrenreich and Ehrenreich 1979), "contradictory class locations" (Wright 1979), "independent primary workers" (Edwards 1979)—typically subsume routinized, non-goods-producing service workers into the former, leaving Poulantzas's position at odds not only with Marx but also with most contemporary Marxists (see also Braverman

1974; Resnick and Wolff 2003). Cherlin, a newcomer to the discussion and by no means a Marxist, provides a pragmatic definition based on secondary characteristics (education) that captures much the same group indicated by these theorists: "Young adults without bachelor's degrees . . . are the would-be working class—the individuals who would have taken the industrial jobs we used to have or married someone who did" (2014, 149).

So if working-class consciousness can plausibly be held by those in frontline jobs, regardless of whether they yield physical goods, what does it in fact consist of? Here the question becomes less sociostructural than political. The distinction between a class "in itself" (a common relation to the means of production) and "for itself" (a common political outlook and organization), long attributed to Marx, has led to considerable focus on what this "for itself" really means. In "The Eighteenth Brumaire of Louis Bonaparte," Marx answers this in a negative sense with respect to "small-holding peasants":

> The identity of their interests begets no community, no national bond, and no political organization among them. . . . They are consequently incapable of enforcing their class interests in their own name, whether through a parliament or through a convention. ([1852] 1972, 516)

Class consciousness here appears as either an appropriate form of organization or a medium of articulation for working-class interests. Ostensibly, these consist in collective ownership and control of the means of production and, barring such revolutionary achievements, the most generous wages, conditions, and social services attainable. A similar interpretation is also supported by Marx's assertion in *The Holy Family* that

> the question is not what goal is *envisaged* for the time being by this or that member of the proletariat, or even by the proletariat as a whole.

> The question is *what is the proletariat* and what course of action will
> it be forced historically to take in conformity with its own *nature*.
> (Quoted in Lukács [1923] 1971, 46, emphasis in original)

Lukács builds upon this conception to further distinguish class
consciousness from what he calls "psychological" consciousness.
To him,

> class consciousness consists in fact of the appropriate and rational ac-
> tions "imputed" [*zugerechnet*] to a particular typical position in the
> process of production. This consciousness is, therefore, neither the sum
> nor the average of what is thought or felt by the single individuals who
> make up the class. ([1923] 1971, 51)

For Lukács class consciousness is not a subjective state held by this
or that person or even articulated in group fashion through cultural practices. It is rather the objective interest of a class as determined by its position in social production and can be imputed
(presumably by intellectuals) or episodically achieved by that class
only in the course of upheaval.

Though forcefully rejected by V. I. Lenin and other Communist
Party builders in the early twentieth century, Lukács's conception
fits neatly with that developed by Lenin in "What Is to Be Done?"

> The history of all countries shows that the working class, exclusively
> by its own effort, is able to develop only trade union consciousness
> [and not] [t]he theory of socialism [which] grew out of the philo-
> sophic, historical, and economic theories elaborated by educated
> representatives of the propertied classes, by intellectuals. ([1903]
> 1975, 24)

On the basis of this analysis, Lenin called for an organization of
"*professional revolutionaries*, irrespective of whether they have developed from among students or working men" that could spread

socialist consciousness among workers (76). Antonio Gramsci's (1971) call for "organic intellectuals" of the working class had a similar bent, and the two levels identified by Lenin—trade union and socialist consciousness—largely correspond with Mann's class identity and opposition, on the one hand, and class totality and alternative society, on the other.

But the gulf between consciousness as objective class interest and our received notion of psychological subjectivity has been too wide for some to bridge. Erik Olin Wright, in empiricist fashion, deploys "class consciousness" as a "strictly micro-concept. . . . Collectivities, in particular class formations," he argues, "do not 'have' consciousness in the literal sense, since they are not the kind of entities which have minds, which think, weigh alternatives, have preferences, etc." (1997, 193). His perspective continues and formalizes a long line of quantitative, survey-based research that usually defines class consciousness as a four- or five-part construct in line with Mann's or Giddens's (1980) formulations (Goldthorpe et al. 1969; Leggett 1968; Zingraff and Schulman 1984; Vallas 1987).

Another group of thinkers also finds the objectivist, "imputational" model unconvincing, but for different reasons. These qualitative and culturally oriented researchers develop their ideas from the work of social historians, E. P. Thompson first among them. "The class experience," he proclaimed,

> is largely determined by the productive relationships into which men are born—or enter involuntarily. Class-consciousness is the way in which these experiences are handled in cultural terms: embodied in traditions, value-systems, ideas, and institutional forms. If the experience appears as determined, class-consciousness does not. We can see a *logic* in the responses of similar occupational groups undergoing similar experiences, but we cannot predicate any *law*. (1963, 9–10, emphasis in original)

For Thompson and his followers, class consciousness neither can nor should be imputed via structural analysis, nor measured in static, "ideational" fashion with attitude questionnaires (Fantasia 1995; see also 1988). Instead it should be interrogated as an empirical, historically unfolding phenomenon that "arises in the same way in different times and places, but never in *just* the same way" (Thompson 1963, 10; see also Katznelson 1986). Taken to its logical conclusion, this perspective advocates an erasure of class consciousness per se, at least in its standardized, abstract form, in favor of grounded qualitative study. Indeed, this is exactly what Fantasia proposes in his article "From Class Consciousness to Culture, Action, and Social Organization" (1995). This perspective has strong parallels in the work of Pierre Bourdieu (1984) who substitutes "habitus" for "consciousness" and sees class—or social position generally—as determined by the intersection of cultural, social, and economic capital.

Class consciousness has thus been defined in three different ways: (1) as an objective set of interests that are achieved or approached through class action at the societal level; (2) as a set of attitudes held by individuals that might incline them to take part in such action; (3) as interpersonal exchange and identity formation among workers in specific contexts. Are these mutually exclusive? On the face of it, they do not appear so. Rather, each way of conceptualizing class consciousness focuses on different aspects of its development. One can stipulate at the level of class relations what working-class interests are and what actions might advance them; one can assess the attitudes of individual workers to see where they stand in relation to these; and one can engage in extended qualitative study to determine the processes that engender consciousness—of whatever form—among actual groups of workers. This book has pursued a combination of the second and the third, but the difference between all three seems to consist more in methodology than in theoretical substance.

Last is the question of which forces enable or inhibit the growth of class consciousness. Is it the workplace? Politics? Cultural ideology? And where do race, gender, and other forms of nonclass oppression fit in? Burawoy (1979, 1985) privileges the workplace. His reasoning is that if capitalism is essentially the appropriation of surplus value, the site of that exploitation is the primary place for its nature to be revealed or concealed. But while this view has clear intuitive merit, observers of the American labor movement—Perlman (1928) first and foremost—as well as of its Russian counterpart, have long implicated political rights or the denial thereof in ameliorating or accentuating class consciousness. Howard Kimmeldorf (1999, 4) refers to the U.S. case as an "unusual combination of political quiescence and industrial revolt" while Louis Althusser ([1962] 2006) famously argued that it was the "overdetermination" of the labor-capital conflict by tsarist repression and a peasant revolt that led to the Bolsheviks' success in Russia. Katznelson (1982) extends the American reasoning further into the realms of race and ethnicity, proposing that these divisions supplied fodder for political disunity among American workers throughout the twentieth century.

A very different school blames cultural ideology for blunting class consciousness. Max Horkheimer and Theodor Adorno (2002, 115) saw in the Hollywood films and pop music of the 1940s a hegemonic "culture industry" that they believed "can do as it pleases with the needs of consumers—producing, controlling, disciplining them". "The masses," they theorized, were being "kept in order by the spectacle of implacable life and the exemplary conduct of those it crushes" (123). Herbert Marcuse (1964), a member of the same Frankfurt school, similarly saw postwar consumerism as engendering "repressive desublimation"—a displacement of working-class grievances into corporatized and equally alienating consumption—while Jürgen Habermas (1984) described this as the "colonization of the lifeworld" by an interlinked capitalist-state "system." Althusser ([1970] 2001) delineated the reproductive role of capital's "ideological apparatuses," (schools, media, the church, etc.) but also thought these could serve as sites of struggle. Overall, the rapid spread of propagandized information in an era of electronic media has been seen by most to weaken working-class consciousness.

More than any other, Michel Foucault has theorized the dynamics of extraeconomic oppression and how it reinforces "bourgeois" domination. He argues that

> from the eighteenth century onward, Western societies created and deployed a new apparatus. . . . I am speaking of the deployment of sexuality . . . linked to the economy through numerous and subtle relays, the main one of which, however, is the body—the body that produces and consumes. (1978, 106–7)

Foucault saw the rise of industrial capitalism as underpinned by a shift from a "society of blood" to a "society of sex." The reproductive function of creating new workers and consumers was no longer left to natural proclivities with power maintained by public displays of state violence but actively pursued through an "incitement to discourse" about "normal" sexual relations that invariably upheld the patriarchal family of male breadwinners and subordinate female caregivers. Thus gender inequality, ingrained at the level of reproduction but extending often enough to wage labor itself (Eisenstein 2010; Milkman 1987), intimately divides workers, privileging men over women and creating a barrier to class solidarity.

W. E. B. DuBois ([1935] 1998), David Roediger (1991), and Manning Marable (1983) describe American race relations in similar terms. Working-class status, they note, has often been associated with whiteness in the United States and seen as a step up from chattel slavery, debt peonage, or urban poverty. Michelle Alexander has influentially updated this perspective for the neoliberal era. "Like Jim Crow (and slavery)," she writes, "mass incarceration operates as a tightly networked system of laws, policies, customs, and institutions that operate collectively to ensure the subordinate status of a group defined largely by race" (2010, 13). The "black undercaste," as she calls it, is a sector of the American working class whose members are far more likely than their white peers to be imprisoned and labeled "felons" (see also Wacquant 2008, 2009).

These internecine divisions, to which one could add nationality, religion, and more, privilege certain segments of the working class over others. They may inculcate a defensive posture among the former that mitigates class consciousness. But the disadvantaged experience even deeper oppression than that of class alone. For some, this may encourage a myopic identity politics; for others, it may heighten their militancy, opposition, and solidarity. Cobble (1991a) documents the "sisterhood" engendered among waitresses that enabled their unionization in the mid-twentieth century; Leon Fink and Brian Greenberg (1989) detail how racial segregation accelerated health care worker organizing in civil rights-era New York; and both Milkman (2006) and Ness (2005) argue that immigrant workers are often among the most class-conscious in their workplaces. Referring to immigrant worker organizing in New York, Ness finds that "class solidarity developed out of the enduring identities workers brought with them from their home countries, their shared experience of workplace oppression, and the racialized identities imposed on them by their employers, the government, and the rest of the segregated city and region" (2005, 185). "Immigrant workers," he concludes, "have a greater propensity to organize and resist oppression on the job than do native-born workers" (186).

Following Burawoy, I focused in this study on the role of the labor process in creating or abating service workers' class consciousness. But I strove not to be tone-deaf to the additional forces—political, racial, sexual, and demographic—that shape it. The retail workers I studied would be accepted by all except Poulantzas (1975) as members of the working class and thus candidates for its imputed or historical consciousness. Although they do not generate surplus value in the strict sense, even Marx would have assigned them to the ranks of workers, since productivity was hardly a criterion for class belonging on his score. And though class consciousness is often conceived as a macrolevel phenomenon embracing the totality of social relations and their political superstructure, it clearly has precursors in the trade-union consciousness of individual workers:

> The collisions between individual workmen and individual bourgeois take more and more the character of collisions between two classes. There upon the workers begin to form combinations (Trades' Unions) against the bourgeois; they club together in order to keep up the rate of wages; they found permanent associations in order to make provision beforehand for these occasional revolts. (Marx and Engels [1848] 1988, 63).

It is the formation and expansion of such clubs, combinations, and associations among service workers, and the provisioning for their future resistance, that this book has explored.

References

Adams, Thomas Jessen. 2006. "Making the New Shop Floor: Wal-Mart, Labor Control, and the History of the Postwar Discount Retail Industry in America." In *Wal-Mart: The Face of Twenty-First-Century Capitalism*, edited by Nelson Lichtenstein, 213–30. New York: New Press.

Aglietta, Michel. 1979. *A Theory of Capitalist Regulation: The U.S. Experience.* New York: Verso.

Alexander, Michelle. 2010. *The New Jim Crow: Mass Incarceration in the Age of Colorblindness.* New York: New Press.

Althusser, Louis. (1962) 2006. *For Marx.* Reprint, New York: Verso.

——. (1970) 2001. *Lenin and Philosophy and Other Essays.* Reprint, New York: Monthly Review Press.

Angotti, Tom. 2008. *New York for Sale: Community Planning Confronts Global Real Estate.* Cambridge, MA: MIT Press.

Appelbaum, Eileen, Annette Bernhardt, and Richard Murnane. 2003. *Low-Wage America: How Employers are Reshaping Opportunity in the Workplace.* New York: Russell Sage.

Aronowitz, Stanley. 1972. *False Promises: The Shaping of American Working Class Consciousness.* New York: McGraw-Hill.

Attewell, Paul. 1987. "The Deskilling Controversy." *Work and Occupations* 14 (3): 323–46.

——. 1990. "What Is Skill?" *Work and Occupations* 17 (4): 422–48.

Barmash, Isadore. 1989. *Macy's for Sale: The Leveraged Buyout of the World's Largest Store.* New York: Weidenfeld and Nicholson.

Becker, Ben. 2014. "Taking Aim at Target: West Indian Immigrant Workers Confront the Difficulties of Big-Box Organizing." In *New Labor in New York: Precarious Workers and the Future of the Labor Movement*, edited by Ruth Milkman and Ed Ott, 25–48. Ithaca, NY: ILR/Cornell University Press.

Bélanger, Jacque, and Paul Edwards. 2013. "The Nature of Frontline Service Work: Distinctive Features and Continuity in the Employment Relationship." *Work, Employment and Society* 27 (3): 433–50.

Bell, Daniel. 1960. *The End of Ideology and the Exhaustion of Political Ideas in the 1950s.* Cambridge, MA: Harvard University Press.

———. 1973. *The Coming of Post-Industrial Society: A Venture in Social Forecasting.* New York: Basic Books.

Benson, Susan Porter. 1986. *Counter Cultures: Saleswomen, Managers, and Customers in American Department Stores, 1890–1940.* Urbana: University of Illinois Press.

Blauner, Robert. 1964. *Alienation and Freedom: The Factory Worker and His Industry.* Chicago: Chicago University Press.

Bluestone, Barry, Patricia Hanna, Sarah Kuhn, and Laura Moore. 1981. *The Retail Revolution: Market Transformation, Investment, and Labor in the Modern Department Store.* New York: Praeger.

Bluestone, Barry, and Bennett Harrison. 1982. *The Deindustrialization of America: Plant Closings, Community Abandonment, and the Dismantling of Basic Industry.* New York: Basic Books.

Bolton, Sharon C. 2005. *Emotion Management in the Workplace.* London: Palgrave.

Bolton, Sharon C., and Carol Boyd. 2003. "Trolley Dolly or Skilled Emotion Manager? Moving on from Hochschild's *Managed Heart*." *Work, Employment and Society* 17 (2): 289–308.

Bolton, Sharon C., and Maeve Houlihan. 2010. "Bermuda Revisited? Management Power and Powerlessness in the Worker-Manager-Customer Triangle." *Work and Occupations* 3 (37): 378–403.

Bourdieu, Pierre. 1984. *Distinction: A Social Critique of the Judgment of Taste.* London: Routledge.

Braverman, Harry. 1974. *Labor and Monopoly Capital: The Degradation of Work in the Twentieth Century.* New York: Monthly Review Press.

Brenner, Aaron, Robert Brenner, and Cal Winslow. 2010. *Rebel Rank and File: Labor Militancy and Revolt from Below in the Long 1970s.* New York: Verso.

Brody, David. 1964. *The Butcher Workmen: A Study of Unionization.* New York: Oxford University Press.

Bronfenbrenner, Kate, ed. 2007. *Global Unions: Challenging Transnational Capital through Cross-Border Campaigns.* Ithaca, NY: ILR/Cornell University Press.

Bronfenbrenner, Kate, Sheldon Friedman, Richard W. Hurd, Rudolph A. Oswald, and Ronald L. Seeber, eds. 1998. *Organizing to Win: New Research on Union Strategies.* Ithaca, NY: ILR/Cornell University Press.

Brook, Paul. 2009. "In Critical Defense of 'Emotional Labour': Refuting Bolton's Critique of Hochschild's Concept." *Work, Employment and Society* 23 (3): 531–48.

Brown, Jenny. 2011. "Rite Aid Warehouse Workers Win Contract after National Push." *Labor Notes*, May 6.

Burawoy, Michael. 1978. "Toward a Marxist Theory of the Labor Process: Braverman and Beyond." *Politics & Society* 8 (3–4): 247–312.

——. 1979. *Manufacturing Consent: Changes in the Labor Process under Monopoly Capitalism*. Chicago: Chicago University Press.

——. 1985. *The Politics of Production: Factory Regimes under Capitalism and Socialism*. New York: Verso.

Burns, Joe. 2011. *Reviving the Strike: How Working People Can Regain Power and Transform America*. New York: IG Publishing.

Cherlin, Andrew J. 2014. *Labor's Love Lost: The Rise and Fall of the Working-Class Family in America*. New York: Russell Sage.

Clawson, Dan. 2003. *The Next Upsurge: Labor and the New Social Movements*. Ithaca, NY: ILR/Cornell University Press.

Chun, Jennifer Jihye. 2009. *Organizing at the Margins: The Symbolic Politics of Labor in South Korea and the United States*. Ithaca, NY: ILR/Cornell University Press.

Cobble, Dorothy Sue. 1991a. *Dishing It Out: Waitresses and Their Unions in the Twentieth Century*. Urbana: University of Illinois Press.

——. 1991b. "Organizing the Postindustrial Work Force: Lessons from the History of Waitress Unionism." *Industrial and Labor Relations Review* 44 (3): 419–36.

Cockburn, Cynthia. 1983. Brothers: Male Dominance and Technological Change. London: Pluto.

Cohen, Liz. 2003. *The Consumer's Republic: The Politics of Mass Consumption in Post-War America*. New York: Vintage.

Coulter, Kendra. 2014. *Revolutionizing Retail: Workers, Political Action, and Social Change*. New York: Palgrave Macmillan.

Cowie, Jefferson. 2010. *Stayin' Alive: The 1970s and the Last Days of the Working Class*. New York: New Press.

Cowie, Jefferson, and Nick Salvatore. 2008. "The Long Exception: Rethinking the Place of the New Deal in American History." *International Labor and Working-Class History* 74 (1): 1–32.

Crompton, Rosemary, and Gareth Jones. 1984. *White-Collar Proletariat: Deskilling and Gender in Clerical Work*. London: Palgrave Macmillan.

Curley, Caitriona, and Tony Royle. 2013. "The Degradation of Work and the End of the Skilled Emotion Worker at Aer Lingus: Is It All Trolley Dollies Now?" *Work, Employment and Society* 27 (1): 105–21.

Darr, Asaf. 2006. *Selling Technology: The Changing Shape of Sales in an Information Economy.* Ithaca, NY: ILR/Cornell University Press.

Davis, Mike. 1999. *Prisoners of the American Dream: Politics and Economy in the History of the U.S. Working Class.* New York: Verso.

DePillis, Lydia. 2014. "Under Pressure, Wal-Mart Upgrades Its Policy for Helping Pregnant Workers." *Washington Post*, April 5.

Dohse, Knuth, Ulrich Jürgens, and Thomas Malsch. 1985. "From 'Fordism' to 'Toyotism'? The Social Organization of the Labor Process in the Japanese Automobile Industry." *Politics & Society* 14 (2): 115–46.

Dublin, Thomas. 1979. *Women at Work: The Transformation of Work and Community in Lowell, Massachusetts, 1826–1860.* New York: Columbia University Press.

DuBois, W. E. B. (1935) 1998. *Black Reconstruction in America, 1860–1880.* Reprint, New York: Free Press.

Early, Steve. 2011. *The Civil Wars in U.S. Labor: Birth of a New Workers' Movement or Death Throes of the Old?* Chicago: Haymarket Books.

Edwards, Richard. 1979. *Contested Terrain: The Transformation of the Workplace in the Twentieth Century.* New York: Basic Books.

Ehrenreich, Barbara, and Jon Ehrenreich. 1979. "The Professional-Managerial Class." In *Between Labor and Capital*, edited by Pat Walker, 5–48. Boston: South End Press.

——. 2013. *Death of a Yuppie Dream.* New York: Rosa Luxemburg Stiftung.

Eisenstein, Hester. 2010. *Feminism Seduced: How Global Elites Use Women's Labor and Ideas to Exploit the World.* Boulder, CO: Paradigm.

England, Paula. 1992. *Comparable Worth: Theories and Evidence.* New York: Aldine de Gruyter.

Erickson, Rebecca J., and Amy S. Wharton. 1997. "Inauthenticity and Depression: Assessing the Consequences of Interactive Service Work." *Work and Occupations* 24 (1997): 188–213.

Estey, Marten S. 1955. "Patterns of Union Membership in the Retail Trades." *Industrial and Labor Relations Review* 8 (4): 557–64.

Fantasia, Rick. 1988. *Cultures of Solidarity: Consciousness, Action and Contemporary American Workers.* Berkeley: University of California Press.

——. 1995. "From Class Consciousness to Culture, Action, and Social Organization." *Annual Review of Sociology* 21 (1): 269–87.

Fine, Janice. 2005. *Workers' Centers: Organizing Communities at the Edge of the Dream.* Ithaca, NY: ILR/Cornell University Press.

Fink, Leon, and Brian Greenberg. 1989. *Upheaval in the Quiet Zone: A History of Hospital Workers' Union, Local 1199.* Urbana: University of Illinois Press.

Fishman, Charles. 2006. *The Wal-Mart Effect: How the World's Most Powerful Company Really Works—And How It's Transforming the American Economy.* New York: Penguin.

Foucault, Michel. 1978. *The History of Sexuality.* Vol. 1. New York: Vintage.

Fourastié, Jean. 1949. *Le grand espoir du XX Siécle: Progrés technique, Progrés économique, Progrés social.* Paris: Presses Universitaires de France.

Frank, Dana. 2001. "Girl Strikers Occupy Chain Store, Win Big: The Detroit Woolworth's Strike of 1937." In *Three Strikes: Miners, Musicians and Salesgirls, and the Fighting Spirit of Labor's Last Century,* edited by Howard Zinn, Dana Frank, and Robin D. G. Kelly, 57–118. Boston, MA: Beacon Press.

Freeman, Joshua B. 2000. *Working-Class New York: Life and Labor since World War II.* New York: New Press.

Fudge, Judy, and Rosemary Owens, eds. 2006. *Precarious Work, Women, and the New Economy: The Challenge to Legal Norms.* Oxford, UK: Hart.

Ganz, Marshall. 2009. *Why David Sometimes Wins: Leadership, Organization, and Strategy in the California Farm Worker Movement.* New York: Oxford University Press.

Giddens, Anthony. 1980. *The Class Structure of Advanced Societies.* London: Hutchison.

Glasmeier, Amy K. 2012. Living Wage Calculator. http://livingwage.mit.edu.

Goldfield, Michael. 1987. *The Decline of Organized Labor in the United States.* Chicago: University of Chicago Press.

Goldthorpe, John H., David Lockwood, Frank Bechhofer, and Jennifer Platt. 1969. *The Affluent Worker in the Class Structure.* Cambridge: Cambridge University Press.

Gordon, David M. 1996. *Fat and Mean: The Corporate Squeeze of Working Americans and the Myth of Managerial Downsizing.* New York: Free Press.

Graham, Laurie. 1995. *On the Line at Subaru-Isuzu: The Japanese Model and the American Worker.* Ithaca, NY: ILR/Cornell University Press.

Gramsci, Antonio. 1971. *Selections from the Prison Notebooks.* New York: International Publishers.

Greenhouse, Steven. 2014. "A Push to Give Steadier Shifts to Part-Timers." *New York Times,* July 15.

———. 2015. "How to Get Low-Wage Workers into the Middle Class." *Atlantic Monthly,* August 19.

Guy, Mary Ellen, and Meredith A. Newman. 2004. "Women's Jobs, Men's Jobs: Sex Segregation and Emotional Labor." *Public Administration Review* 64 (3): 289–98.

Habermas, Jürgen. 1984. *The Theory of Communicative Action*. Vol. 1. Boston: Beacon Press.

Halle, David. 1984. *America's Working Man: Work, Home, and Politics among Blue-Collar Property Owners*. Chicago: University of Chicago Press.

Hampson, Ian, and Anne Junor. 2010. "Putting the Process Back In: Rethinking Service Sector Skill." *Work, Employment and Society* 3 (24): 526–45.

Harrington, Michael. 1962. *The Retail Clerks*. New York: Wiley.

Hartmann, Heidi. 1981. "The Unhappy Marriage of Marxism and Feminism: Towards a More Progressive Union." In *Women and Revolution*, edited by Lydia Sargent, 1–41. Boston: Beacon Press.

Harvey, David. 2005. *A Brief History of Neoliberalism*. New York: Oxford University Press.

———. 2006. *The Limits to Capital*. New York: Verso.

Heckscher, Charles. 2001. "Living with Flexibility." In *Rekindling the Movement: Labor's Quest for Relevance in the Twenty-First Century*, edited by Lowell Turner, Harry Katz, and Richard W. Hurd, 59–81. Ithaca, NY: ILR/Cornell University Press.

Henly, Julia R., H. Luke Shaefer, and Elaine Waxman. 2006. "Nonstandard Work Schedules: Employer- and Employee-Driven Flexibility in Retail Jobs." *Social Service Review* 80 (4): 609–34.

Hirschman, Albert O. 1970. *Exit, Voice, and Loyalty: Responses to Decline in Firms, Organizations and States*. Cambridge, MA: Harvard University Press.

Hirsch, Barry, and David Macpherson. 2014. "Union Membership and Coverage Database from the CPS." http://unionstats.com/.

Hochschild, Arlie. 1983. *The Managed Heart: Commercialization of Human Feeling*. Berkeley: University of California Press.

Hodson, Randy. 1996. "Dignity in the Workplace under Participative Management: Alienation and Freedom Revisited." *American Sociological Review* 5: 719–38.

Hoopes, James. 2006. "Growth through Knowledge: Wal-Mart, High Technology, and the Ever Less Visible Hand of the Manager." In Lichtenstein, *Wal-Mart*, 83–104.

Horkheimer, Max, and Theodor W. Adorno. 2002. *Dialectic of Enlightenment: Philosophical Fragments*. Stanford, CA: Stanford University Press.

Hurd, Richard W. 2008. "Collective Bargaining in the Era of Grocery Industry Restructuring." Articles and Chapters, no. 284. http://digitalcommons.ilr.cornell.edu/articles/284.

Ikeler, Peter. 2014. "Infusing Craft Identity into a Noncraft Industry: The Retail Action Project." In *New Labor in New York: Precarious Workers and* the Future of the Labor Movement, edited by Ruth Milkman and Ed Ott, 113–33. Ithaca, NY: ILR/Cornell University Press.

Jacobs, Ken, Ian Perry, and Jenifer MacGillvary. 2015. "The High Public Cost of Low Wages." UC Berkeley Labor Center Research Brief. http://laborcenter. berkeley.edu/pdf/2015/the-high-public-cost-of-low-wages.pdf.

Jacoby, Sanford M. 1997. *Modern Manors: Welfare Capitalism since the New Deal*. Princeton, NJ: Princeton University Press.

Jenkins, Steve. 2002. "Organizing, Advocacy, and Member Power: A Critical Reflection." *WorkingUSA: The Journal of Labor and Society* 6 (2): 56–89.

Jessop, Bob. 1982. *The Capitalist State: Marxist Theories and Methods*. Oxford, UK: Martin Robinson.

Jones, Andrew. 2001. "Caring Labor and Class Consciousness: The Class Dynamics of Gendered Work." *Sociological Forum* 16: 281–99.

Juravich, Tom, and Kate Bronfenbrenner. 2005. "Introduction: Bringing the Study of Work Back to Labor Studies." *Labor Studies Journal* 30 (1): i–vii.

Kalleberg, Arne L. 2000. "Nonstandard Employment Relations: Part-time, Temporary, and Contract Work." *Annual Review of Sociology* 26: 341–65.

———. 2011. *Good Jobs, Bad Jobs: The Rise of Polarized and Precarious Employment Systems in the United States, 1970s to 2000s*. New York: Russell Sage.

Kasinitz, Philip, John H. Mollenkopf, Mary C. Waters, and Jennifer Holdaway. 2008. *Inheriting the City: The Children of Immigrants Come of Age*. New York: Russell Sage.

Katznelson, Ira. 1982. *City Trenches: Urban Politics and the Patterning of Class in the United States*. Chicago: University of Chicago Press.

———. 1986. "Working-Class Formation: Constructing Cases and Comparisons." In *Working-Class Formation: Nineteenth-Century Patterns in Western Europe and the United States*, edited by Ira Katznelson and Aristide R. Zolberg, 3–41. Princeton, NJ: Princeton University Press.

Kimmeldorf, Howard. 1999. *Battling for American Labor: Wobblies, Craft Workers and the Making of the Union Movement*. Berkeley: University of California Press.

Kirstein, George C. 1950. *Stores and Unions: A Study of the Growth of Unionism in Dry Goods and Department Stores*. New York: Fairchild.

Kochan, Thomas A., Harry C. Katz, and Robert B. McKersie. 1994. *The Transformation of American Industrial Relations*. Ithaca, NY: ILR/Cornell University Press.

Korczynski, Marek. 2002. *Human Resource Management in Service Work*. Basingstoke, UK: Palgrave Macmillan.

Lambert, Susan J. 2008. "Passing the Buck: Labor Flexibility Practices That Transfer Risk onto Hourly Workers." *Human Relations* 61: 1203–27.

Leach, William. 1993. *Land of Desire: Merchants, Power, and the Rise of a New American Culture.* New York: Vintage.

Lebhar, Godfrey M. 1952. *Chain Stores in America: 1859–1950.* New York: Chain Store Publishing.

Leggett, John C. 1968. *Class, Race, and Labor: Working-Class Consciousness in Detroit.* New York: Oxford University Press.

Leidner, Robin. 1993. *Fast Food, Fast Talk: Service Work and the Routinization of Everyday Life.* Berkeley: University of California Press.

Leidner, Robin. 1996. "Rethinking Questions of Control: Lessons from Mc-Donald's." In *Working in the Service Society,* edited by Cameron Lynne MacDonald and Carmen Sirianni, 29–49. Philadelphia: Temple University Press.

———. 1999. "Emotional Labor in Service Work." *Annals of the American Academy of Political and Social Science* 561 (1): 81–95.

Lenin, V. I. (1903) 1975. "What Is to Be Done? Burning Questions of Our Movement." In *The Lenin Anthology,* edited by Robert C. Tucker, 12–114. New York: Norton.

Lerner, Stephen S. 2011. "A New Insurgency Can Only Arise outside the Progressive and Labor Establishment." *New Labor Forum* 20 (3): 9–13.

Levinson, Marc. 2011. *The Great A&P and the Struggle for Small Business in America.* New York: Hill and Wang.

Lichtenstein, Nelson. 1982. *Labor's War at Home: The CIO in World War II.* New York: Cambridge University Press.

———, ed. 2006. *Wal-Mart: The Face of Twenty-First-Century Capitalism.* New York: New Press.

———. 2009. *The Retail Revolution: How Wal-Mart Created a Brave New World of Business.* New York: Holt.

Lipietz, Alain. 1989. *Towards a New Economic Order: Post-Fordism, Ecology, Democracy.* New York: Oxford University Press.

Lopez, Steven Henry. 2004. *Reorganizing the Rustbelt: An Inside Study of the American Labor Movement.* Los Angeles: University of California Press.

———. 2010. "Workers, Managers, and Customers: Triangles of Power in Work Communities." *Work and Occupations* 37 (3): 251–71.

Luce, Stephanie. 2004. *Fighting for a Living Wage.* Ithaca, NY: ILR/Cornell University Press.

Lukács, Georg. (1923) 1971. *History and Class Consciousness: Studies in Marxist Dialectics.* Reprint, Cambridge, MA: MIT Press. Citations refer to the 1971 edition.

Macy's. 2012a. "Macy's, Inc. Annual Report 2012." http://www.macysinc.com/Assets/docs/for-investors/annual-report/2011_ar.pdf.

——. 2012b. "Macy's, Inc. Factbook 2012." http://www.macysinc.com/assets/docs/for-investors/annual-report/2012_fact_book.pdf.

Mann, Michael. 1973. *Consciousness and Action among the Western Working Class.* London: Macmillan.

Marable, Manning. 1983. *How Capitalism Underdeveloped Black America.* Cambridge, MA: South End Press.

Marcuse, Herbert. 1964. *One-Dimensional Man.* Boston: Beacon Press.

Marx, Karl. (1852) 1972. "The Eighteenth Brumaire of Louis Bonaparte." In *The Marx-Engels Reader,* edited by Robert C. Tucker, 436–525. New York: Norton.

——. (1867) 1976. *Capital.* Vol. 1. Reprint, New York: Penguin. Citations refer to the Penguin edition.

——. (1893) 1981. *Capital.* Vol. 3. Reprint, New York: Penguin. Citations refer to the Penguin edition.

Marx, Karl, and Friedrich Engels. (1848) 1988. *The Communist Manifesto.* Reprint, New York: Norton. Citations refer to the Norton edition.

Mayo, James. 1993. *The American Grocery Store: The Business Evolution of an Architectural Space.* New York: Greenwood.

McCallum, Jamie K. 2013. *Global Unions, Local Power: The New Spirit of Transnational Labor Organizing.* Ithaca, NY: ILR/Cornell University Press.

Miles, Kathleen. 2013. "Largest Civil Disobedience in Walmart History Leads to More than 50 Arrests." *Huffington Post,* November 8. http://www.huffingtonpost.com/2013/11/08/walmart-arrests_n_4227411.html.

Milkman, Ruth. 1987. *Gender at Work: The Dynamics of Job Segregation by Sex during World War II.* Urbana: University of Illinois Press.

——. 1991. *Japan's California Factories: Labor Relations and Economic Globalization.* Los Angeles: Institute of Industrial Relations, University of California, Los Angeles.

——. 2004–5. "Win or Lose: Lessons from Two Contrasting Union Campaigns." *Social Policy* (winter): 43–47.

——. 2006. *L.A. Story: Immigrant Workers and the Future of the U.S. Labor Movement.* New York: Russell Sage.

——. 2013. "Back to the Future? US Labour in the New Gilded Age." *British Journal of Industrial Relations* 51 (4): 645–65.

Mills, C. Wright. 1951. *White Collar: The American Middle Classes.* New York: Oxford University Press.

Monaghan, David, and Peter Ikeler. 2014. "Global Centrality and Income Inequality in U.S. Metropolitan Areas: A Test of Two Hypotheses." *Sociological Focus* 47 (3): 174–93.

Montgomery, David. 1979. *Workers' Control in America: Studies in the History of Work, Technology and Labor Struggles*. New York: Cambridge University Press.

———. 1987. *The Fall of the House of Labor: The Workplace, the State, and American Labor Activism, 1865–1925*. New York: Cambridge University Press.

Moody, Kim. 1988. *An Injury to All: The Decline of American Unionism*. New York: Verso.

———. 1997. *Workers in a Lean World*. New York: Verso.

———. 2007. *US Labor in Trouble and Transition: The Failure of Reform from Above, the Promise of Revival from Below*. New York: Verso.

Moreton, Bethany. 2009. *To Serve God and Wal-Mart: The Making of Christian Free Enterprise*. Cambridge, MA: Harvard University Press.

National Retail Federation. 2013. "Top 100 Retailers: The Nation's Retail Power Players 2012." https://nrf.com/resources/top-retailers-list/top-100-retailers-2013s.

Ness, Immanuel. 2005. *Immigrants, Unions and the New U.S. Labor Market*. Philadelphia: Temple University Press.

Nickson, Dennis, Chris Warhurst, Johanna Commander, Scott A. Hurrell, and Anne Marie Cullen. 2012. "Soft Skills and Employability: Evidence from UK Retail." *Economic and Industrial Democracy* 33 (1): 65–84.

O'Grady, John. 1995. *Job Control Unionism vs. the New Human Resources Management Model*. Kingston, ON: IRC Press.

Ohno, Taiichi. 1988. *Toyota Production System: Beyond Large-Scale Production*. New York: Productivity Press.

Opler, Daniel J. 2007. *For All White-Collar Workers: The Possibilities of Radicalism in New York City's Department Store Unions, 1934–1953*. Columbus: University of Ohio Press.

Penn, Roger. 1986. "Where Have All the Craftsmen Gone?: Trends in Skilled Labor in the United States of America since 1940." *British Journal of Sociology* 37 (4): 569–80.

Perlman, Selig. 1928. *A Theory of the Labor Movement*. New York: A.M. Kelly.

Picketty, Thomas. 2014. *Capital in the Twenty-First Century*. Translated by Arthur Goldhammer. Cambridge, MA: Belknap/Harvard University Press.

Piore, Michael, and Charles Sabel. 1984. *The Second Industrial Divide: Possibilities for Prosperity*. New York: Basic Books.

Piven, Frances Fox, and Richard A. Cloward. 1979. *Poor People's Movements: Why They Succeed, How They Fail*. New York: Vintage Books.

Poulantzas, Nicos. 1975. *Classes in Contemporary Capitalism*. London: NLB.

Preis, Art. (1964) 1972. *Labor's Giant Step: The First Twenty Years of the CIO: 1936–55.* 2nd ed. New York: Pathfinder. Citations are to second edition.

Resnick, Stephen, and Richard Wolff. 2003. "The Diversity of Class Analyses: A Critique of Erik Olin Wright and Beyond." *Critical Sociology* 29 (1): 7–27.

Reutschlin, Catherine. 2012. *Retail's Hidden Potential: How Raising Wages Would Benefit Workers, the Industry, and the Overall Economy.* New York: Demos.

Ritzer, George. 1993. *The McDonaldization of Society.* Thousand Oaks, CA: Pine Forge Press.

Roediger, David R. 1991. *The Wages of Whiteness: Race and the Making of the American Working Class.* New York: Verso.

Rosen, Ellen Israel. 2006. "How to Squeeze More out of a Penny." In Lichtenstein, *Wal-Mart*, 243–60.

Rowley, Laura. 2003. *On Target: How the World's Hottest Retailer Hit a Bull's-Eye.* Hoboken, NJ: Wiley.

Sabel, Charles. 1982. *Work and Politics: The Division of Labor in Industry.* Cambridge, MA: MIT Press.

Sassen, Saskia. 2001. *The Global City: New York, London, Tokyo.* 2nd ed. Princeton, NJ: Princeton University Press.

Schlosser, Eric. 2001. *Fast Food Nation: The Dark Side of the All-American Meal.* New York: Houghton Mifflin.

Sennett, Richard, and Jonathan Cobb. 1972. *The Hidden Injuries of Class.* New York: Norton.

Sherman, Rachel. 2007. *Class Acts: Service and Inequality in Luxury Hotels.* Berkeley: University of California Press.

Silver, Beverly. 2003. *Forces of Labor: Workers' Movements and Globalization since 1870.* New York: Cambridge University Press.

Slaughter, Jane. 2012. "Strikes at Walmart Warehouses Expose Threats in Supply Chain." *Labor Notes*, September 24.

Sloan, Melissa M. 2007. "The 'Real Self' and Inauthenticity: The Importance of Self-Concept Anchorage for Emotional Experiences in the Workplace." *Social Psychology Quarterly* 70 (2007): 305–18.

Smith, Adam. (1776) 1993. *An Inquiry into the Nature and Causes of the Wealth of Nations.* Selected ed. New York: Oxford University Press. Citations are to Oxford edition.

Smith, Vicki. 1998. "The Fractured World of the Temporary Worker: Power, Participation, and Fragmentation in the Contemporary Workplace." *Social Problems* 45 (4): 411–30.

——. 2001. *Crossing the Great Divide: Worker Risk and Opportunity in the New Economy*. Ithaca, NY: ILR/Cornell University Press.

Spector, Robert. 2005. *Category Killers: The Retail Revolution and Its Impact on Consumer Culture*. Cambridge, MA: Harvard Business Review.

Spenner, Kenneth. 1983. "Deciphering Prometheus: Temporal Changes in the Skill Level of Work." *American Sociological Review* 48: 824–37.

Standing, Guy. 2011. *The Precariat: The New Dangerous Class*. New York: Bloomsbury.

Strasser, Susan. 2006. "Woolworth to Wal-Mart: Mass Merchandising and the Changing Culture of Consumption." In Lichtenstein, *Wal-Mart*, 31–56.

Tabuchi, Hiroko. 2015. "Walmart Raising Wage to at Least $9." *New York Times*, February 19.

Tannock, Stuart. 2001. *Youth at Work: The Unionized Fast-Food and Grocery Workplace*. Philadelphia: Temple University Press.

Target Corporation. 2008. "Team Member Handbook—Target Stores Non-Exempt."

——. 2012a. "History." https://corporate.target.com/about/history.

——. 2012b. "Target 2011 Annual Report." http://investors.target.com/phoenix.zhtml?c=65828&p=irol-reportsannual.

——. 2013. "Target Careers—College Students." https://corporate.target.com/careers/college-students.

Taylor, Phil, and Peter Bain. 1999. "'An Assembly Line in the Head': Work and Employee Relations in the Call Centre." *Industrial Relations Journal* 30 (2): 101–17.

Thompson, E. P. 1963. *The Making of the English Working Class*. New York: Vintage.

Tilly, Chris. 1996. *Half a Job: Bad and Good Part-Time Jobs in a Changing Labor Market*. Philadelphia: Temple University Press.

Tolich, Martin B. 1993. "Alienating and Liberating Emotions at Work: Supermarket Clerks' Performance of Customer Service." *Journal of Contemporary Ethnography* 22 (3): 361–81.

Tonelson, Alan. 2002. *The Race to the Bottom: Why a Worldwide Worker Surplus and Uncontrolled Free Trade Are Sinking American Living Standards*. Boulder, CO: Westview Press.

U.S. Bureau of Labor Statistics. 2005. "Economic News Release: Contingent and Alternative Employment Arrangements, February 2005." http://www.bls.gov/news.release/conemp.nr0.htm.

——. 2014a. "Current Employment Statistics." http://bls.gov/ces/data.htm.

——. 2014b. "Current Population Survey." http://www.bls.gov/cps/.

——. 2014c. "Labor Productivity and Costs." http://bls.gov/lpc/#data.

———. 2014d. "Occupational Employment Statistics." http://www.bls.gov/oes/.

Vallas, Steven P. 1987. "The Labor Process as a Source of Class Consciousness: A Critical Examination." *Sociological Forum* 2: 237–56.

———. 2003. "Why Teamwork Fails: Obstacles to Workplace Change in Four Manufacturing Plants." *American Sociological Review* 68 (2): 223–50.

Veblen, Thorstein. 1899. *The Theory of the Leisure Class.* New York: Macmillan.

Voss, Kim, and Rachel Sherman. 2000. "Breaking the Iron Law of Oligarchy: Union Revitalization in the American Labor Movement." *American Journal of Sociology* 106 (2): 303–49.

Wacquant, Loïc. 2008. *Urban Outcasts: A Comparative Sociology of Advanced Marginality.* Malden, MA: Polity.

———. 2009. *Punishing the Poor: The Neoliberal Government of Social Insecurity.* Durham, NC: Duke University Press.

Walsh, John P. 1991. "The Social Context of Technological Change: The Case of the Retail Food Industry." *Sociological Quarterly* 32 (3): 447–68.

Wharton, Amy S. 1993. "The Affective Consequences of Service Work." *Work and Occupations* 20 (2): 205–32.

Whitfield, Keith. 2000. "High-Performance Workplaces, Training, and the Distribution of Skills." *Industrial Relations: A Journal of Economy and Society* 39 (1): 1–24.

Womack, James P., and Daniel T. Jones. 2003. *Lean Thinking: Banish Waste and Create Wealth in Your Corporation.* New York: Free Press

Wood, Stephen. 1987. "The Deskilling Debate, New Technology and Work Organization." *Acta Sociologica* 30 (1): 3–24.

Wright, Erik Olin. 1979. *Class Structure and Income Determination.* New York: Academic Press.

———. 1997. *Class Counts.* Student ed. New York: Cambridge University Press.

———. 2000. "Working-Class Power, Capitalist-Class Interests, and Class Compromise." *American Journal of Sociology* 105 (4): 957–1002.

Zingraff, Rhonda, and Michael D. Schulman. 1984. "Social Bases of Class Consciousness: A Study of Southern Textile Workers with a Comparison by Race." *Social Forces* 63 (1): 98–116.

Ziskind, Minna P. 2003. "Labor Conflict in the Suburbs: Organizing Retail in Metropolitan New York, 1954–1958." *International Labor and Working-Class History* 64 (2): 55–73.

Zukin, Sharon. 2004. *Point of Purchase: How Shopping Changed American Culture.* New York: Routledge.

Index